Social Equality
THE CHALLENGE OF TODAY

Rudolf Dreikurs, M.D.

ADLER SCHOOL OF PROFESSIONAL PSYCHOLOGY

Copyright © 1971 by Rudolf Dreikurs
Second Printing 1983
Third Printing 1990
Fourth Printing 1994
Fifth Printing 2000
Library of Congress Catalog Card No. 83-72318

ISBN 0-918560-30-6

Adler School of Professional Psychology, Inc.
65 East Wacker Place, Chicago, IL 60601

Manufactured in the United States of America

*To Rodney, Beth, Bruce, Linda,
my grandchildren,
with my fervent hope that they may
live in a world of equality, justice,
and peace.*

२।१२।२०१३

CONTENTS

ACKNOWLEDGMENTS

I wish to acknowledge the invaluable contributions of Ross Allen McClelland, whose editorial suggestions were incorporated.

My special thanks to my dearest wife who, with wise guidance, wrote this book with me.

R.D.

PREFACE

Man is a social being. His basic desire is to belong. Only if one feels one belongs can one function, participate, contribute. Alfred Adler described this basic human desire as *Gemeinschaftsgefuehl,* which can be roughly translated as social interest, a sense of communion, of feeling that one is embedded in the stream of life, of concern for the welfare of others. The degree of a person's social interest determines his ability and willingness to function socially; the lack of social interest is at the root of deficiencies, failures, and pathology. Thus, Adler found that social interest was a gauge for defining normalcy, both for the individual and for the group. This gauge permits the measuring not only of the individual but of society itself. For this reason Adler considered social interest as a challenge to mankind.[1]

Adler postulated an "Ironclad Logic of Social Living"—a basic law that governs all social transactions, as the law of gravity governs all movements of physical bodies, be they stars or movements on earth. This basic social law is similar to the law of gravity. The gravitational pull on earth forces everything that goes up to come as far down as possible. Regardless of how high a spring is, its water has to come down to the level of the ocean, and nothing can stop the flow for any great length of time.

---

1. Alfred Adler, *Social Interest: A Challenge to Mankind* (London: Faber & Faber, 1938).

Similarly, throughout our civilization, whenever a group set itself up as superior, it created instability; sooner or later it had to come down and be replaced by another dominant group. Adler recognized equality as a fundamental prerequisite for the logic of social living; without it, there can be no stability or social harmony.

This book can be considered a sequel to Adler's book on social interest. The challenge is to establish social equality for all, particularly in our time when the democratic evolution, itself a consequence of man's search for social peace and harmony, permits everyone—at least everyone in the United States—to consider himself as equal to everyone else.

As social interest is decisive for the function of each individual, so a sense of social equality is a prerequisite if everyone is to develop his social interest. Yet the concept of social equality is difficult to grasp. It becomes the challenge of *today* —as never before in history. Only a society of equals can build democracy, and democracy is the dominant characteristic of a new phase of mankind's experience.

What we currently are experiencing are the birthpains of a new society: hardship, confusion, and turmoil. But there is no ill caused by the democratic evolution that cannot be cured by more democracy. Many have tried to resolve the predicament by turning the clock back to the "good old days." Hitler tried it in vain, and no aspiring dictator will fare any better. We simply have to learn how to live with each other as equals. This is the paramount challenge of our generation. It may well be the factor that determines whether western society will survive or collapse. We have the ability to accomplish either. The future of mankind hangs in the balance.

INTRODUCTION

We have reached a state in our civilization at which man has established his mastery on this earth to an extent that would have been unbelievable to men of past generations. We could be ready to enter paradise, perhaps for the first time in the history of mankind. There is plenty for everyone. We have the productive capacity to provide for all men whatever food and goods they want and need. This is no longer a dream of utopia; it is reality. Or it could be reality . . . *if* . . . . This *if* does not depend on technical or scientific progress: Man's ingenuity has solved most of the technical problems of living. The *if* is a question of whether we can apply our technical discoveries and achievements.

Paradise *could* be attained if man only knew how to apply his knowledge for the benefit of all. Is the technical and scientific progress, which has accelerated in geometric progression since the beginning of this century, useless? Is it worth the sweat and blood and sacrifice of those who brought it about? Could we be just as satisfied with a primitive form of living where lives were short and men were the victims of the elements and the pawns of the natural forces? What good is all this progress if it does not help us to live in peace with each other and with ourselves?

Few will deny that most of us feel alarmed and threatened, particularly those of us in the United States, the "land of plenty." Turmoil and strife, insecurity and fear are the furies of modern times. We may go through life looking undisturbed, but few of us have experienced the deep serenity of which philosophers spoke and poets sang—the inner contentment in living, the fulfillment of our aspirations and spiritual strivings. Is mankind incapable of such a life? Is the Tower of Babel to be an eternal symbol of man's inability to reach the stars or to make a heaven on earth?

I cannot agree with this pessimistic conclusion, which the contemporary picture seems to support and justify. Yet man, who has learned so much, still does not know some of the fundamental requirements of social living. He cannot live at peace within his family; nor does he know how to raise his children. He cannot enjoy his life without intoxication, without rushing madly to acquire, to accomplish, to get somewhere. Unselfish love has become a lost art; faith in anything, an outdated notion; relaxation, an idle dream. Man has become his fellow man's worst enemy, and the closer we live to each other, the more we fight and fear each other. We are worse off than were our ancestors, who were well acquainted with autocratic methods and who, under their system, knew what to do and why. The traditional methods of dealing with interpersonal problems are no longer effective. The new methods necessary for social living in a democratic atmosphere are hardly known, at least to the vast majority of our contemporaries. Most modern people do not know—nor do they believe when they are told—that democracy presupposes a relationship of equals, the recognition of a fundamental human equality. Therefore, they cannot treat each other as equals and cannot solve their problems on the basis of mutual respect. How can one be optimistic when confronted with all this?

Yet there are grounds for optimism, for this distress in the midst of plenty is not accidental. On the contrary, it indicates an important stage in the *progress* of civilization. We are standing at the doorstep of a new cultural era.

Our present turmoil does not indicate that man has learned nothing through the centuries. Rather, the intensification of our social tensions and conflicts constitutes the beginning of a new era. We may call our present age the Age of Anxiety. We may call it the Atomic Age. But actually it is the beginning of the Age of Democracy. And what distinguishes the democratic era from the autocratic past is the change in interpersonal and intergroup relationships from those of dominance and submission to those of equality.

Today a husband and wife cannot live peacefully with each other if they do not treat each other as equals. Nor can parents get along with their children if they assume that their children can be subdued. There can be no harmony and stability in the community unless each member of it has his safe place as an equal to all others. There can be no cooperation between management and labor unless each group feels respected and trusted by the other. There can be no peace on earth unless one nation respects the rights and dignity of another. There can be no harmony as long as there is no voluntary agreement, because force can no longer solve conflict or controversy.

In fact, we are in an interregnum, so to speak. Our society is no longer autocratic; we have a deep revulsion against autocratic methods. And yet we are not familiar with what even the existing degree of democracy requires from each of us individually and from all of us collectively in order that we may profit from a democratic society.

At the personal level a man who earnestly seeks perspectives for living sees himself as physically weak, a tiny mote within the overwhelming multiplicity of galaxies, and faces many perplexing questions: What am I? Have I a purpose? Have I a destiny? Is there a reason for my being within this vast universe? Is not a feeling of significance in such circumstances mere vanity? In nearer relationships within my world, my country, my community, my social circle, my family, my work, what are my obligations? How can I meet their daily challenge? Why do so many people fail to find happiness? Why is frustration so common? How can I feel the impact of those nearest to me? What can I do in the face of hostility and aggression, to say nothing of the clash of temperaments? What of my rights, my morals, my personal dignity? Do these exist, or must I establish them for myself by virtue of personal power or clever choice of allies? Is there a general philosophy by which I may guide my steps that will serve to further my happiness and the happiness of all dear to me?

We need guidelines in this confusing world of ours. We need a new orientation in a scene that has drastically changed, a scene in which a new concept of the universe is emerging, different from what scientists believed even a few decades ago.

Democratic evolution made man the agent responsible for himself, and for the sphere in which he operates. Man is no longer a servant: he is the master of himself. But unaccustomed to his new role in society, man does not sense his mastery. He has not yet become aware of either his full potentialities or his actual strength. Nor does he recognize the status as a social equal that a democratic society bestows upon him. In his fear of being inferior, he tries to establish his superiority over others. He cannot recognize others as his equals at a time when they really are. He is a free agent, but he does not feel free. He must discover himself in order to find personal peace and to live at peace with others.

This is the challenge of today.

Part I

THE DISCOVERY OF SELF

CHAPTER 1 · **The Inner Shackles**

To a large degree we determine our destiny and invite our fate. Daily, for better or worse, we prepare our own porridge —more often, for worse, for we prepare it without knowing that we are doing it and in ignorance of most of the resources we could muster for doing it better. In most of us, most of the time, the short-sighted pygmy-self is in control. We tragically underestimate our abilities and, consequently, allow the larger portion of them to "rust in us unused," while we writhe in a wretchedness that could promptly be relieved by knowledgeable, confident self-assertion. Some people use their faculties more than do others, but it is doubtful if many use as much as 25 percent of the talent and energy available to them.

What is it that weighs us down, holds us back, and makes it almost impossible to imagine what each of us could do and be? Prejudice against ourselves is one thing; a faulty notion of human nature in general and of ourselves in particular is another; but the main stumbling block in the way of our knowing and using our great inner resources is our *lack of belief in our own strengths and abilities.*

The almost inconceivable control that we all possess over *all* our faculties, physical, emotional, or intellectual, becomes indisputably visible under hypnotic influence. In such cases we attribute the power to the hypnotist, but, actually, the hypnotist does nothing but convince the subject of his own ability to produce the desired results. It is the subject's conviction that counts. Anyone who is convinced can achieve the same control over all his functions as the hypnotist's sub-ject demonstrates. We need no hypnotist or "healer" to do the "miraculously" unexpected; we need only the belief that we can do it.

Naturally, all of us are constrained by the conditions of our existence and influenced by the incidents in our lives. Some-times these conditions provide us with opportunities to rec-ognize and experience our real capacities, and sometimes they seem to deprive us of this chance. Yet it is not conditions themselves that are of importance but our reactions to them, the way we experience them. We "make" our experience, which we use as we see fit. Our responses can turn danger into accomplishment or, contrariwise, opportunity into defeat.

In fact, we not only influence the conditions under which we live, we often actually produce them. More important still, *we determine the meaning* of any circumstance to which we are exposed. We decide the stimulation to which we will respond.

We are not pawns of fate or victims of our environments, as we are told: we alter conditions, create situations, influence people, invite the responses we get. Above all, each of us ex-periences whatever occurs in a very special personal way and makes a very special personal use of the experience.

THE IMPORTANCE OF SELF-CONCEPT

The moving force behind all our actions is an inner plan, according to which we act and which we hardly know. Our attitudes toward others and toward life depend on what we think of ourselves. This fundamental truth has far-reaching consequences. We can respect others only if we respect our-selves and trust life only if we trust ourselves. Our self-con-cepts shape all our interests, strivings, feelings, and move-ments. If we accept ourselves as we are, we do not waste energy fighting with ourselves. This "saved" energy is then available for coping with the contingencies of life around us. *We ourselves are our greatest problem.* We must first make peace with ourselves. Then we can turn to the rest of the world with confidence, courage, and often joy.

We all know people who seem to be blessed with good luck and others who are apparently bedeviled by failure and misfortune. When we closely examine the "lucky bird" or "fall guy," however, we find personal patterns peculiar to each. The first is quite sure of his ability and expects to succeed. Consequently, he sizes up each situation properly and acts in accordance with its needs. He knows when to be aggressive and when to bide his time, when to talk and when to keep silent. As a result, he is usually successful in what he tries. Sometimes, however, he, too, fails. Then, instead of fretting, making excuses, or placing blame, he simply reexamines his approach, corrects it, and succeeds. When his goals are beyond his present opportunity to achieve, he waits for a better occasion and occupies himself in the meantime with other problems. In the end, everything seems to turn out well for him.

The second *expects* to fail *before* he even starts; hence, he is nervous and tense. In his anxiety, he misjudges the situation and therefore fails to act in accordance with its demands. He is aggressive when he should wait, quiet when he should talk. As a result, he fails—as he had expected to do. He makes his own bad dream come true. Then he gives up. Yet even he may occasionally meet with "success." This sudden turn disturbs him. It doesn't fit his plan; it compels him to reexamine the situation until he has finally confused the issue once more. Then he can fail again, and again, and again. It is his attitude that causes his defeats. But he cannot accept that explanation. He feels justified in his pessimism because of his many bad experiences. He *thinks* he wants to see success before he will believe in his ability to succeed—he won't go near the water until after he's learned to swim. In fact, even if he were to accomplish a great deal, it would be of little avail. For success in itself would not provide him with a belief in his own strength and ability. He would dismiss the achievement as accidental. Only when he changes his opinion of himself can his behavior change. As long as he thinks he is a failure he will "succeed" in proving that he is.

We all create experiences to "prove" what we think we are, to fit our self-concepts. But what are we, really?

KNOWING OURSELVES

That every man needs to take account of himself is not a new idea. "Know thyself" has been a standard prescription ever since Socrates proclaimed it as both an ideal and an obligation for a responsible man. Today especially our dissatisfaction with ourselves has made us increasingly introspective. We look within, but we don't know what to look for. We are more confused than ever as to what we can know of ourselves and what we cannot. Progress in the behavioral sciences has produced considerable information about our psychological processes, about our inner workings, but it has also produced confusion about contradictory conclusions. An eager public devours a vast literature, enrolls in numerous classes, and attends many lectures on human motivation in general, hoping to gain some clues, yet becoming more bewildered and perplexed.

How much self-knowledge can we acquire? Some people suggest we should examine our emotions in order to control them; others want to modify our behavior. Neither group gives us insight into our goals, concepts, and intentions. It is questionable whether we should or even could find out what we are. Yet many people waste their time and energy trying to do just that. They do not know that in order to know what we are, we have to *forget* ourselves. Only then can we "find ourselves"; only in doing do we express what we are.

But what we are, what qualities and properties we possess, is less important than what we do with what we have. What he is born with is less important to a child than what he does with his talents afterward. Our psychology is one of "use" and not of "possession."

We may neglect to develop great potential abilities, or we may reach the highest level in an area where we have previously experienced an innate deficiency. Present performance is not a measure of potential or a determinant of future performance. In most cases we grossly underestimate our abilities.

What can we know about ourselves? Can we analyze our emotions, or perhaps our dreams? Some think so. But there is reason to doubt that this really can be done. We may know our thoughts and feelings; use them to "explain" our actions. But the real reasons for our actions—our intentions—remain unrecognized most of the time, particularly if we try to justify inadequate actions or deficiencies.

And so we go on, unaware of our strengths and impressed with our limitations. What we know and can do is taken for granted; only what we cannot do is exaggerated and desirable.

THE PREJUDICE AGAINST OURSELVES

Our habitual underestimation of ourselves is both a cause and a consequence of deep-seated inferiority feelings. The important question therefore becomes: Can we overcome our inferiority feelings, our assumption of not measuring up? If so, what means can we use? First, it is necessary to recognize inferiority feelings as a *prejudice against ourselves*. We *assume* that we are inferior because of our original faulty self-appraisals. Then we become afraid that some assumed or real (but overestimated) deficiency may be discovered by others. We nervously harbor guilty secrets, although we are not quite certain what those secrets are. Finally, we reconfirm our poor opinion of ourselves time and time again, while busily trying to hide our inadequacies from others. We repeat the same mistakes to "verify" our low self-estimates, although they may contradict common sense and reality.

Fortunately, an understanding of the dynamics of the process by which we cause our dark predictions to come to pass and then use our failure as a basis for making further dark predictions points to a method for escaping this sorry cycle, for lessening inferiority feelings and increasing self-esteem.

Mere argument is futile in overcoming prejudices. Everyone has worked out logical reasons to support his prejudice and can back up his logic with strong emotions. Prejudice can, however, be overcome, and many triumphs have been reported. The first prerequisite is that we become aware that we are prejudiced; the second is that we become willing to reconsider the facts upon which the prejudice is based; the third is that we become aware that we have more to gain from changing our opinions than from keeping them. Only if we can visualize a possible change of heart can the process of reexamining the facts have a favorable outcome.

Just as these processes can be applied to the fight against class, racial, sexual, or religious prejudice, they also fit into our fight against inferiority feelings; that is, the prejudice against ourselves. Every form of psychotherapy tries to correct this prejudice, although some therapeutic methods may attack the problem in a roundabout way. The basic element in any "cure" or improvement, regardless of the method employed—science, religion, or whatever—is the elimination of inferiority feelings, the restoration of the patient's faith in himself. Any effective therapy or "healing" provides a sense of strength and importance, essential to well-being and adequate functioning.

ARE WE GOOD ENOUGH?

Why do we find it so hard to believe that our assumption of inferiority is only a "prejudice"? Our rigidity in this regard is easy to explain. As children we learned that we were not "good enough" as we were. Only if we earned better grades, learned more, did better, gained special skills and abilities—only then could we hope to "amount to anything," to "be worthwhile." Our traditional educational pattern stresses a negative value: hardly anyone is good enough *as he is*. We perpetuate this pernicious practice under the fallacious assumption that growth and improvement demand dissatisfaction with oneself. Admittedly, in some few cases the drive for self-evaluation *may* stimulate progress. But in all cases this negative urge is unnecessary, and in many cases it is highly detrimental.

The devotees of travail are mistaken: learning and growth *can* be fostered through joyful activity, through enthusiastic participation and usefulness, through play and pleasurable efforts. Anyone who is sure of himself and satisfied with his abilities can do *better* than someone who must constantly struggle to prove his worth. Of course, one might well ask, cannot the fear of not measuring up lead to the successful application of compensatory efforts? To this I would answer, Yes—but *only* within a restricted field in which one already *believes* in his abilities. It is the feeling of adequacy, rather than of inadequacy, that leads to successful endeavor.

For what reasons, then, do we usually assume that believing in oneself is a detriment to growth and that doubt is an essential stimulus? Most of us take our skills that are already developed for granted and attach more importance to those that we lack. In this way we maintain our fear of being deficient. We are proud of our own accomplishments only to the point of bolstering our own endangered egos and think that any new endeavor may expose our deficiencies. Thus, we can never enjoy our present abilities and current stages of development because there is always so much ahead of us, and along that road ahead there is no sign reading "Final Success."

There *is* never any final success. The solution of one problem gives rise to another. And each new problem becomes a new "test" of our ability and worth. We react as we did to the ever-repeated and increasingly difficult tests at school. As our parents and teachers continually weighed and measured us in our early days, we continually weigh and measure ourselves today. What are we worth? Well, we really don't know till the next grades are posted, and after that the next grades, *ad infinitum.* Our value is forever in doubt, forever in need of reaffirmation.

What nonsense! Human worth is independent of incidental activity. Unfortunately, few of us know this. We have been duped into trying to judge ourselves in accordance with tomorrow's honor roll or dunce cap, and we rather suspect it will be the latter. This constant doubt of our ability to "measure up" the next time begins to be regarded as evidence that we really *are* inferior; hence, we make no serious effort to rid ourselves of inferiority feelings.

The first step in escaping from inferiority feelings, then, is recognition of the fact that we have a prejudice against ourselves. The second step requires that we ask ourselves again and again: "Am I *really* inadequate or insufficient?" For those who regard anything less than perfection as inadequate, this question is repugnant. Such people lack the "courage to be imperfect." Yet perfection is an Utopian myth; it has no existence in reality. Everything done by anyone could be done better by someone else. Is everyone, therefore, inadequate? The greatest achievements of the most outstanding geniuses were eventually improved upon by others. Does that make the original contributions less worthwhile? *Whatever we contribute is useful.* Usefulness alone gives meaning to life. But our prestige-hungry generation is not satisfied merely with being useful. We have to be "better," and what we do must be better. Otherwise we think we are failures.

SUCCESS AND FAILURE

Discarding the contemporary obsession with success and failure is the third step toward freeing ourselves from assumptions of inferiority. No one can be sure of continuous success; no one is insured against failure. Yet we feel that our social positions are so insecure that we are deadly afraid of making mistakes. But it is only human to make mistakes; it is humanly impossible to avoid making them. Naturally, we should make a reasonable effort to avoid making mistakes, but lack of belief in our ability to avoid humiliating mistakes and fear of consequences are responsible for many unnecessary errors. We all move in the direction of our anticipations, pleasant or painful.

If we could take our mistakes in our stride without fear of *losing status,* we would be equipped to perform better and would actually make fewer mistakes. In any case, it is less important *what* mistakes we make than *what we do* after we have made them. If we do not allow ourselves to be discouraged, ashamed, or humiliated, we may use our resources to correct our errors, sometimes with better results than if all had gone well from the start.

Conversely, we place too high a premium on "success." The emphasis on success and the horror of failure go together: our concern with success impedes our performance because it threatens us with failure. Instead of merely doing our best and "keeping our eyes on the ball," we are distracted by a preoccupation with the prestige that might be shattered if we are not successful. We lose the joy of living, the pleasure of doing things. Although we think our concern stimulates our abilities, it actually lessens them, and worry confines our satisfaction to those rare and fleeting instants when great success is achieved. The injection of the issue of success or failure into any activity makes the activity a hazard. As soon as someone diverts his attention from any task to ask, "How am I doing?" he takes his concern and energy from the task and shifts them to the question of his own adequacy or deficiency. The best motivation for doing a job well is the satisfaction of doing it.

Alfred Adler always advised his medical students: Do your job as well as you can and let the chips fall as they may, without having a personal stake in the success or failure. If you try to be especially successful, Adler said, you become a servant to your patients in order to demonstrate your ability.

A man who is bent on *proving* his value will inevitably find that he has none: he already doubts his own value, or there would be no need for proof. And as he doubts his value, he injects his preconceived low opinion of himself into whatever he encounters. Even when he is successful, he will be impressed less by his accomplishments than by an occasional slip. We all are impressed primarily by those experiences that "prove" what we already believe. A vain woman ignores the many men who pay her compliments to fret over the one who ignores her.

Attempts to prove one's value are altogether futile. No proof can bring lasting self-confidence to anyone who doubts himself; no circumstance can be too trivial to serve as a testing ground for the uncertain. An uncertain person can find "tests" of his ability even in functions that lie within the reach of every human being—sleeping, thinking, signing his name. Then his concern with himself disturbs these simple functions: he cannot sleep, think well, or write his name without trembling. Defective performances become convincing evidence of his deficiency.

When we look at ourselves as we are, or rather as we think we are, it seems absurd to assume that we shall ever be really free. To be free of frequent doubts and fears, to be free to feel and think and act spontaneously—what a lovely dream! And how soon that dream is interrupted by "reality"! To move more freely in a broader, brighter world would seem to require some deep and basic change, not just in ourselves, but in the entire human species. The unlikelihood of such a transmutation is our nightmare.

After all, have we not tried, and tried hard, to overcome our weaknesses and eliminate our faults? And where has it left us? Right back where we were before: deficient and self-defeating, unwilling or unable to do what we know would be best for us and for others. As to mankind, look where it is today: we are no better adjusted socially than were the citizens of the first great cities thousands of years ago, with crime rampant and wars raging, in a dog-eat-dog society no more harmonious than that of the earliest civilizations. The bitter and often bloody social and political strife that stains the pages of all recorded history is no mere dream, nightmarish though it may be; neither is the personal suffering so poignantly recorded in our music and poems.

Is violent conflict, then, a part of human nature? And was Burns correct in stating, "Man was made to mourn"? Can we influence the social order and ourselves for the better? The answer—*our* answer—determines whether we stand on the brink of catastrophe or at the threshold of a new cultural era.

CAN WE INFLUENCE OURSELVES?

To be sure, mankind as yet has not fulfilled the promises of Micah and the other prophets of peace and accord, and we all fall short of what we could be. We betray our own ideals and are socially delinquent in many ways. While most of us try earnestly to "improve" ourselves, we meet with very little success. Does this mean that self-improvement is difficult, almost to the point of being impossible? Or could it be that our relative lack of success is a result of faulty self-improvement methods? It seems that we simply are not able to grow in the direction we desire; therefore, we repeatedly defeat ourselves. Perhaps the outcome of our efforts to "take ourselves firmly in hand" would have been quite different had we learned in the first place just *how* to treat ourselves.

The question of how we treat ourselves takes on a new dimension in this age of increasing democratization, when we no longer rely upon authorities to tell us what to do and to "make us toe the line." We know now that what the authorities told us to do was most often in their own self-interest. What most of us don't know, however, is that the *methods* by which they made us toe the line have utterly lost their effectiveness. Promises and threats, bribes and punishment, the chief control techniques of aristocracy and of its heir-in-disguise, authoritarianism, no longer work. To offer a good conduct medal to an equal is insulting; to punish him is outrageous. Let us imagine an identical twin who says to his brother, "If you are a good boy today, I'll give you a lollipop tonight; if you are a bad boy, I'll give you a spanking." In an age when all except the privileged demand social equality, we refuse to accept the assumed superiority of those who would appoint themselves dispensers of lollipops and spankings.

Ironically, although we do not respond favorably to such high-handed methods, we try to apply them to our children. And even more ironically, we try to apply them to ourselves.

We say such things as, "If I keep my New Year's resolutions till spring, I'll allow myself to buy a camper. If I make a fool of myself at the party tonight, I won't allow myself to go fishing." And, more generally, "I shall take myself firmly by the scruff of the neck and *make* myself straighten up and fly right." Therein lies our failure. The method is obsolete. We can no longer *make* anyone, even our children and ourselves, do anything. To influence anyone successfully—our colleagues, our children, or ourselves—we must change our influence methods to match the changing times. And whomever we wish to influence, we will use the same new techniques.

Many of the new, workable techniques have already been developed, but, unfortunately, knowledge of them is not as yet widespread. It is likely that future generations will be better prepared to live in a truly democratic atmosphere, when these new approaches and concepts, expanded and refined, will have become common knowledge. But we can live more fully and freely in our time by learning and applying *today* those principles of democratic interaction and influence already discovered and described by Alfred Adler, his followers, and other humanistic psychologists.

A word of warning is in order here. If a person's basic personality is in need of analysis and change, expert outside help is essential. A meaningful reexamination of self-concepts, life style, and motivations is impossible without such help. Nevertheless, a wide range of improvements in our functioning can be brought about through a new psychological orientation. To assist in this reorientation is one of the major objects of this book.

Traditionally, it has been held that there is a curious dichotomy in the human personality; it is as if the personality consists of different and often opposing parts. These "parts" are seen as acting independently because they *seem* to act that way. Mind and body seem to go their separate ways: "The spirit is willing but the flesh is weak." Reason and emotion seem to sabotage each other; the conscious and the unconscious never seem to meet; code and conduct appear to disagree. Subjectively we can reconfirm such theoretical assumptions. We frequently have the sensation of being torn apart by the forces within ourselves, and the tendency to see opposing forces everywhere, especially within ourselves, is further reinforced by the prevailing moralistic concept of good and bad, exemplified by our ideas of God and the Devil. Present psychoanalytic theories also support such concepts. In the Freudian model of man the Super-ego and the Id, as well as the conscious and the unconscious, are identified with the good and bad in man, and the poor Ego is placed in between, to be battered this way and that from above and below.

It is impossible to gain an appropriate, workable picture of ourselves as long as we continue to think in this traditional dualistic way. Yet such an appropriate, workable picture is essential to the next step toward greater inner freedom and the resulting "self-improvement": self-acceptance. Self-acceptance does not imply resignation or stagnation; it refers to the acceptance and enjoyment of "being" on the way to "becoming." To accept ourselves as we are, we must realize that everything in us is part of us, not foreign to us; that *we* are responsible for everything that goes on in us; that we can direct these things; and, moreover, that we *do* direct them—*all* the time.

We use our minds and our bodies, our thoughts and our emotions, every part of our beings, for the purposes that *we* have set for ourselves. *We even decide what we want to know and what to conceal from our full awareness.* How could we possibly "repress" unacceptable urges and thoughts if we didn't know which ones they were? But, unfamiliar as we are with the totality of our individual existence, we identify ourselves only with the more highly conscious thoughts and feelings. These we consider as "the real us." We set up a hierarchy within ourselves, in which we experience some parts of ourselves as strictly "us," other parts more remotely so, and still others as altogether alien to us. This makes it hard for us to perceive fully that *a man is, indeed, in command of all that is within him all of the time, that his "ego" is in control of everything.* Although our bodies can be affected by outside causes, can become diseased and injured without our wills' saying so, our regenerative forces do not operate "naturally" —that is, automatically—as some mechanistic thinkers assume. The forces of nature within us are mobilized by *us; we* direct them to be detrimental or beneficial. We can lie down and die whenever we decide to. And when we *really* want it, that is precisely what we will do. Conversely, we can win a battle for life, against extremely heavy odds—when we really want to.[1]

We are just beginning to realize the great command we have over mind and body. Unfortunately, the theory behind modern consideration of the unity of man is often mistaken. Psychosomatic medicine, for example, still assumes that there is a dichotomy between mind and body and often neglects the unity of the individual, seeing *forces,* not the person, as the moving agents. Emotional forces are supposed to influence the physiological processes, and vice versa, as if such forces can work by themselves. The theory doesn't make sense when broken down, but superficially there is some truth in it. It is interesting to note that some religious approaches to healing, such as those of Christian Science, show firm grasp of the totality of the individual, although the formulations are not in scientific language. Christian Scientists attribute the cure

---

1. The power to decide life and death is clearly demonstrated by the way the aborigines in Australia carry out a death sentence of an offender. The chief points a kangaroo bone at him with the pronouncement that in three days he will die. And, we are told, the offender dies within three days.

to divine intervention; translated into more realistic terms, what Christian Science calls divine power can be identified as man's own inner resources.

Holistic medicine, as distinguished from psychosomatic medicine, provides a new picture of the integration of all functions within the organism. The whole is more than the sum total of all its parts; no partial phenomena can explain the function of the whole.

We have not developed to the extent of being able to use holistic medicine, however. Therefore, we must accept for the time being a dualistic terminology as a necessary concession to our tendency to assume that there are separate parts within ourselves, ranged in pairs, one of which can deal with the other. The term "influencing ourselves" presupposes that each of us has two such parts. As long as we operate on such assumptions, we seek ways to "deal with ourselves," to "get along with ourselves," to "make peace with ourselves." As long as we can have "attitudes" toward ourselves, our attitudes are decisive in furthering or stifling the use of our inner resources. Ultimately, all effective means of furthering the use of our resources will, directly or by implication, depend upon each person's full identification with his whole organism. The effectiveness or ineffectiveness of a method of dealing with ourselves can be gauged by the direction the method takes: Does it lead each of us toward greater awareness of being one unit, undivided and indivisable? Or does it lead toward concentrating on separate and isolated parts of each personality, driving a wedge between the "conscious" self and the rest? *Whatever increases a man's feeling of wholeness increases his ability to function and to feel well; whatever increases a man's sensation of being composed of various and opposing elements, of forces of good and bad, endangers his well-being and his performance and prevents the full use of his inner resources.* We can use this test to observe our attitudes toward ourselves and to judge which ones need to be reconsidered.

FIGHTING WITH OURSELVES

Most people who are dissatisfied with themselves—and which of us is not at times?—get involved in a futile and dangerous fight. They try to "control" themselves. When these efforts fail—as we have seen they must—the frustrated victims try more desperately and fail more painfully until the ensuing vicious cycle leads to utter demoralization and a deep conviction of insufficient "willpower." This foredoomed Tantalus-like struggle is born of several fallacious presumptions.

Our attempts at self-control originate in childhood, when we are first advised to "control ourselves." Parents and educators, following the autocratic tradition, attempt to establish within the child a vicarious power to carry out their demands, a conscience strong enough to suppress antisocial impulses. Thus self-control becomes an extremely important value. The underlying fallacy is difficult to detect, for self-control *seems* at times to be effective. Do we not at times wrestle our evil angels to the ground and emerge victorious and "virtuous"? Of course we do. But in these instances, we could be "virtuous," anyway, without the sham battle and victory. *Efforts at self-control are successful only when no such efforts are needed.* Our pseudo-struggles, which to us seem very real, conceal the simple fact that we follow our consciences only when we are willing to do so, only when we have decided to act "properly." Otherwise, our efforts to control ourselves are empty gestures, designed merely to make us look "good" both before and after being "bad." We repeatedly reenact an ancient drama, hallowed in Western religion and literature: resist—yield—repent. In our private dramas the appearance of good intentions serves our self-delusion well. Good intentions are mimed in the first act as heroic struggle and in the third act, as abysmal guilt. We develop guilt feelings to express good intentions that we do not have. We would rather blame ourselves than mend our ways. In our ignorance of the fact that all of us, children and adults alike, are doing only what we decide to do, we fail to realize that doing right as we see it requires no self-control, only a *sincere* intention. Lack of self-control distinguishes pretended intentions from real ones.

The emphasis on control reflects another basic misconception. Just as parents need to distinguish between control and influence in training their children, we need to make the same distinction in dealing with ourselves. Whenever we try to control ourselves, we are operating on an outmoded model of man, an obsolete and useless notion of human nature. We display a lack of faith in ourselves, as if something in us is unreliable and "inferior." It is futile to try to control the alien inferior in ourselves, *for there is none.* As a free agent and as a completely integrated and articulated single unit, each of us does what he prefers to do at the time, acting not necessarily on common sense or conscience, but on a private logic, of which we shall say more later.

The sooner we realize this fact of self-direction, which recognizes man as a decision-making organism, the better equipped we shall be to influence ourselves. A person who "lets himself go" is doing what he wants as much as a person who restrains his "objectionable" impulses. To assume that unless we control ourselves we will do horrible things expresses a cultural demoralization, a complete lack of faith in man.

Some people condition themselves to behave properly in "tempting" situations only after they have gone through a violent pantomime of self-control. The occasional success of such control confounds the issue. These people never seem to know why they succeed at one time and fail at another, but the occasional success seems to justify their approach. Actually, the occasional success of self-control is a clever scheme: by "proving" the existence of such control, it provides an excuse for the many occasions when control seems to fail. Then one can blame one's failure on a lack of willpower.

Actually, there is no such thing as willpower. Within the limitations of a given situation, everyone has the power to do what he decides to do. But the assumption that willpower exists, and in different degrees in different persons, is such an efficient servant to chicanery and sham that we find it difficult to give it up. The pretense enables us to do what we should not do and at the same time plead innocent because we are just not "strong enough" to do otherwise. But is a weak person really weak? It requires little psychological sensitivity to see that the so-called weak person puts all the strong people around him in his service. Weakness is one of the *strongest* means of rebellion, defiance, and demand. Regardless of how strong his opponents are, the weakling resists them and makes them do his bidding rather than submit to theirs.

Weakness of will is a deceptive façade. So is strength of willpower. The latter merely provides a display of superiority, something to brag about, to be proud of. He who successfully controls himself wants to demonstrate his superior human quality, to set himself up as an example of strength (now a favorite masculine goal since men have been hard-pressed to prove their superiority to women).

The confusion concerning willpower arises because we have failed to distinguish between what we think we want and what we really want, between what we appear to be trying to do and what we actually intend to do. *True intention is revealed by acts.* We can always tell what we wanted to do by observing what we did.

Take the case of a woman who sees a spring coat she

"wants." She goes into the store, tries it on, and finds it fits her perfectly. It is her dream coat. Then she hears the price. She realizes that she would have to sacrifice a needed refrigerator, or even her summer vacation, to get the coat. She thinks it over. After an inner struggle she decides not to buy it. But whenever she passes this store and sees the coat in the window, her "heart bleeds."

Does she want the coat? She certainly would like to have it. But under the conditions that she could have it, *she does not want it,* although she still would like to have it. Her *decision* indicates what she really wants; her *intention* is evident in her actions. There is neither occasion nor need for self-control. If she were willing to pay the price, she would buy the coat: do what she wants. So it is for all of us. If we decide to pay the price, then we are willing to do what our common sense or our conscience may tell us *not* to do. One can even cut off one's nose, as the old saying goes, to spite one's face!

What we so often experience as inner conflict is not that between what we want to do and what we should do but that between what is to be gained at what price from alternative courses of action. Our estimate of which course is more advantageous decides the issue. The "fight with ourselves" is a mock battle, a "sideshow," as Adler called it, wherein we pretend innocence and good intentions. A simply analogy demonstrates the absurdity of such an "inner struggle."

Try to grasp one hand with the other and pull the left arm to the right side *with all of your strength.* The harder you pull, the less the arm will move. If you want to move your left arm to the right, you can do so with ease, but not with force. *Forcing presupposes holding back at the same time.* There can be no powerful pull without a powerful counter-pull.

In dealing with ourselves we can experience the feeling of strength only if we, at the same time, are exerting an opposing pull. This fact holds true for all functions. The more strongly we "force" ourselves, the less we can do what we supposedly want to do.

The implications for everyday living are far-reaching. Many of our deficiencies are the direct result of our mistaken use of force with ourselves. All neurotic symptoms are established and maintained through fighting them, for whatever we try to suppress in ourselves is thereby enhanced. We may spend a sleepless night because we feel stimulated or are concerned with a problem, but insomnia does not begin until we try to force ourselves to fall asleep. This is why nervous symptoms, once they start, are difficult to overcome. To begin with, they are unconsciously "arranged" in a crisis situation when we wish to withdraw from certain tasks; from then on we try to rid ourselves of a disturbance by *fighting against it*. And thus we strengthen the symptoms. An anecdote may illustrate this point.

Once there was a famous sorcerer who could turn stone into gold, water into wine or milk, one animal into another, and even men into animals. The king, hearing about him and his great magic, invited him to his palace. He wined and dined the sorcerer and took him to his private chambers. There he asked the sorcerer whether the stories about him and his magic were true.

"They are," said the sorcerer.

"I should like," said the king, "to learn this magic. Could I?"

"That depends."

"If it is a question of the price," said the king, "I am willing to give you half of my kingdom."

The sorcerer considered that satisfactory. "But there is another condition for learning this magic."

Eagerly, the king expressed his willingness to meet any condition.

"Do you ever think of a crocodile?" asked the sorcerer.

No, the king did not.

"That is fine," said the sorcerer, "because this is the only condition under which you can learn the magic; namely, never to think of a crocodile."

Needless to say, the king never learned the magic. All he could think about from then on was a crocodile.

This story illustrates the consequences of any attempt to "control our thoughts" by fighting with ourselves. All nervous disturbances are created and maintained in this way; they promptly subside if we can persuade the patient to produce or intensify the symptoms. This process, which I call "anti-suggestion," brings dramatic results, not only in therapy, but in many situations where we try, unsuccessfully, to influence ourselves.[2]

One cannot overestimate the importance of this process. It demonstrates the tremendous power that we have over all our functions, if we only know how to exert this influence. All we have to do is to do the opposite of what we have been doing. The solution is so simple and yet so revolutionary that we often cannot believe the mastery we have over our actions and emotions.

This strange power was first discovered in regard to sea and motion sickness. If you promise to reward a person each time he gets sick, he never "can" get sick.

A group of young children was taken on a bus ride. Many of them had previously suffered from motion sickness on a similar ride. This time each was promised a dollar whenever he got sick. None did.

Then we found out that the same principle applies to all neurotic symptoms. For example, a patient who suffered from insomnia was told to see whether he could stay awake every night for a whole week. When he came in the next week, he reported that, to his great surprise, he had slept every night.

---

2. Viktor Frankl called this mechanism "paradoxical intention," and Knight Dunlap, "negative practice."

He couldn't understand what had happened since before he had spent many nights without shutting his eyes.

Sometimes this technique backfires when a person tries to benefit from an ailment.

A young boy who stammered severely found himself on a bus without any money. Finally, the boy went to the driver, expecting that the driver would pity him when he saw his condition and would let him ride without paying. But when he went up to the driver, the boy found he could not stammer.

THE FALLACY OF FEAR

The most frequent stimulator of the noxious fight with ourselves is fear, fear of what might happen if we were unable to control our mental and physical functions.

Fear and anxiety seem to preoccupy most of our contemporaries, at least in metropolitan areas. That we are indeed a generation of frightened people few will deny, but, they add, are we not justified in being afraid? Who could be aware of all the economic uncertainties, the political upheavals, the constant threat of war and destruction and not be frightened?

Actually, as great as the dangers may be, we feel less threatened by them than by the prospect of possible personal failure, with its catastrophic consequences upon our social status. It has been proven beyond doubt that actual danger seldom produces any sensation of fear. Threat to life and property can be experienced without any fear reaction. Uncertainty about our future successes and about our ability to maintain our status in the community causes the widespread anxiety that is characteristic of modern living.

It is assumed that fear is necessary to avoid dangers. Actually, the opposite is true. Fear increases rather than diminishes the probability of danger. One does not need to fear being hit by an automobile in order to cross a street safely. However, a person who is afraid is more likely to incur such an accident. Fear deprives us of the poise, the ability to make a clear evaluation of a situation, that is necessary in moments of danger. But we must differentiate between *actual danger* and the *thought* of it. Fear is common when we think of possible future perils; even past experiences still may make us shudder. Likewise, we may be extremely frightened when we see someone else in danger. But when we ourselves are in danger, fear usually does not appear; we cannot afford it. It is the thought of danger that evokes fear, be it before or after the frightful experience.

A German poem tells the story of a man who lived on the Bodensee, a large lake between Germany, Austria, and Switzerland. He urgently needed a doctor for a sick child in the middle of the night. So he got on his horse to ride to the next town. Heavy snow obscured the road, and he became lost. Then he saw a light in the far distance. He spurred his horse on to go as fast as he could and finally he reached the house with the light. When he realized that he had crossed the frozen lake, he dropped dead.

In moments of sudden catastrophe we may respond with a *shock* reaction. But this by itself is remote from any sensation of fear; rather, one is stunned and paralyzed. Under certain circumstances, this moment of shock may be utilized to maintain a neurotic fear. Its function is not related, however, to the original cause, but to the ensuing life conditions from which an individual may wish to withdraw. (This is the typical mechanism in "battle fatigue.")

Another emotional reaction to a dangerous situation is *panic*. The prevalence of panic reaction seems to contradict our statement that danger does not evoke fear. Danger *can* evoke panic with certain people and under special circumstances, but they then respond with panic even to situations of no real danger. Such people operate on the assumption that they have to control everything in order to be safe. They cannot trust anyone other than themselves, and they even doubt their own ability to take care of themselves. Consequently, they respond with panic to any situation that "gets out of control." In most instances, the real danger is the consequence, rather than the cause, of the panic reaction. Anticipation of disaster may bring about panic—which in turn may lead to destruction.

Panic indicates a conviction of inevitable catastrophe. Some people experience panic constantly, because they encounter so many situations they cannot control, and they feel lost. However, anyone is susceptible to panic when he finds himself in a hopeless situation, where escape seems impossible.

Another observation may lead to the false impression that fear enhances our ability to avoid danger. Many people are negligent and oblivious to possible dangers unless they are thoroughly shaken up by fear; only then do they become concerned and alert. Many drivers become careful only after they have witnessed or experienced accidents—and then often not for too long. Experienced actors often do their best only if they have stage fright; what prevents others from performing altogether becomes for them a most important stimulant. Does this not disprove the assumption that fear never pays? It pays to those who need it—*by their own decision and choice.* Such actors are not willing to give their best *unless* their audience is a challenge to them. Only if their reputation is at stake are they willing to do their part conscientiously and with enthusiasm. They *utilize* the assumption of a possible danger for their own purpose.

This brings us, then, to the use that people in general make of their ability to be frightened. First, we have to distinguish between the actual experience of fear and a verbal expression: "I am afraid that . . ." This latter phrase expresses concern more than fear and as such is indicative of a normal outlook. Fear, in contrast, is not normal, and like any other strong emotion, it functions primarily in interpersonal relations.

Fear is a weapon that is employed at some time or other by practically all children. Children find it easiest to enlist the parent's help by emphasizing their own weakness. A spoiled child with little confidence in his own powers may be easily alarmed and give way to wild panic the moment the slightest burden is laid on him, though the burden may amount to no more than being left alone for a short while. This feeling is different from the shock reaction that an infant may exhibit as a result of experiencing a loud noise or a sudden loss of support; neither noise nor loss of support will lead to a fear reaction unless the parents are "duly" impressed with a child's predicament and make so much fuss that the child discovers "fear" as a perfect means to get the parents' continued attention and service. It has been clinically shown that fears in children disappear when the parents stop being impressed and no longer respond to them, and these tests disprove the assumption that fear in children is "caused" by a sense of insecurity or by actual frightening experiences.[3] If the assumption were true, the fear would not disappear as completely and permanently as it does when the parents recognize fears as demands for attention and service and refuse to respond.

Fear serves as an effective way of evading difficult tasks that threaten status; it is the basis for every neurosis and it is widely utilized within the normal range of human activities. It either generates special effort and preoccupation or leads to detours, withdrawals, or increased demands for sympathy and support. Moreover, while we all suffer from fear and believe that we want to free ourselves from it, we—at times— take full advantage of our ability to generate fear. Actually, many people become quite concerned at the prospect of losing

---

3. Case histories are presented in Rudolf Dreikurs and Vicki Soltz, *Children: The Challenge* (New York: Hawthorn Books, 1964).

their fears. They imagine the horrible things that would happen if people, including themselves, stopped being afraid.

This brings us to the real source of fear, to its true significance as a social institution. We are thoroughly conditioned to be afraid—not by nature, but by our fellow man. Our response to and dependency on the emotion of fear is part of an autocratic tradition. In an autocratic society fear was used deliberately and systematically to keep the people in line with the demands of the ruling group. Fear of punishment was considered the only reliable means to assure cooperation and submission. If the powers on earth did not provide sufficient intimidation, the powers in heaven were called upon to supply it. Fear was considered the best stimulation for proper behavior. In line with the prevailing low opinion of human nature, man was not considered capable of "behaving" himself unless he was fear-bound, threatened with punishment. Today the old authorities are gone; our parents and teachers have long ceased to threaten us. Yet we continue to threaten ourselves and visualize punishment of one kind or the other as a means of keeping ourselves in line with our own ideals and standards. We have become free from outside suppression and intimidation, but we maintain our slave mentality, not without taking advantage of our self-intimidation by using it to avoid responsibility and to increase our demands—the so-called dependency needs—on others.

Originally it was fear of "sin" that kept man from being "bad." Today it is becoming increasingly obvious that the "sin" of modern man is fear itself. Fear deprives him of his ability to function. It strengthens his convictions about his inherent weakness and deficiency. Fear is the result of his doubt that he can take care of himself on his own strength. But taking care of himself is exactly the obligation of the free man, and he cannot discharge his obligation unless he knows that he can trust himself. Fear of punishment denies

us the confidence that we can be good because we want to be
and not because we are afraid of the consequences of being
bad.

Yet there is joy and satisfaction to be had in doing right.
A sense of responsibility no longer needs to be instilled by
fear. Man is able to behave properly through a feeling of belonging, an awareness of his interrelatedness, the sureness
of his own place, and his full worth as a person.

THE POWER OF EXPECTATION

The full impact of fear becomes evident when we realize
the role of expectations and anticipations, our strongest—
and strangest—motivating forces. *Anyone who can alter the
expectations of people can change their behavior.*

We all act in accordance with our expectations. They form
the secret plan that guides all our actions. We may not know
it or recognize that we have a plan at all. It makes little
difference whether we anticipate events with pleasure or horror; as long as we expect them, we move toward them. Only
when our goals are constructive do we admit them to ourselves, but distressing expectations have the same motivating
effect, even though we are not aware of our direction. Whatever we consider as *probable,* pleasant or painful, establishes
in our mind a plan of movement toward its realization. This
is why fear is so dangerous. Fortunately, what we expect does
not always happen because outside forces sometimes inter-
vene; but our inner resources are geared toward such events,
whether we hope for them or fear them. The power of hypnosis can be explained by the hypnotist's ability to create new—
and often almost incredible—expectations in his subject. The
hypnotist—surrounding himself with mystical powers—is
merely a supersalesman who convinces his clients of the inevitability of his predicted or demanded performance.

Simple examples can demonstrate the power of anticipation. We can easily walk along a board one yard wide when it is placed on the ground. If the same board is suspended high above ground, however, we may hesitate to walk on it, anticipating disaster, and if we attempt the task, we may actually lose our balance and fall. We blame such an event on some "inability," on our nervousness, and so forth, But our "ability" in this case depends not at all on where the board is placed; it depends on our self-evaluation, on our belief or doubt in our ability, on our expectation.

We can increase our effectiveness by familiarizing ourselves with our expectations. We can explore what we anticipate, although it may not always be easy. And before further damage is done, we can reason with and convince ourselves that we do not have to move in the assumed direction. But we can do so only if we become convinced that we are not cornered, that we have chances, although we can spoil them by faulty anticipations. We can improve our judgment by recognizing our ability to produce more favorable effects, to win and to succeed where we had been convinced of inevitable failure. Such recognition involves an improved opinion of ourselves.

SELF-ENCOURAGEMENT

We cannot maintain a sound plan of action unless we put ourselves on a sound basis first. As long as we presume that we are inferior or deficient, we cannot help but expect the worst from ourselves and from life. Our opinion of ourselves, more than anything else, molds our expectations of our future possibilities and limitations. If we are self-confident, we expect success and can bring it about. If we doubt our ability, we anticipate failure and move toward it. *Our self-evaluation is the premise upon which we act.*

It is well known that success begets success, since it increases self-confidence. For those who have success, problems that persist for the timid and dubious vanish. Our self-assurance is reinforced by the reassurance of others and by the effects of our courageous actions.

Self-encouragement in dealing with ourselves is clearly important. Unfortunately, most people treat themselves as strict and severe parents and teachers treat a "bad" child—and with the same negative results. Long after they leave their parents, children carry with them, incorporated in their consciences, the demands made upon them when they were children. They may have rebelled against a domineering mother or father, but they continue to treat themselves as their parents did.

Regardless of the reasons, when we discourage ourselves, we diminish our efficiency. Encouragement is as necessary an obligation in dealing with ourselves as in dealing with anyone else. Consequently, we need the ability and willingness to see our good points and to avoid concentrating on our deficiencies. Everyone has deficiencies, but to emphasize them makes them worse. We may think that we need self-criticism in order to improve ourselves and to avoid making the same mistake again, but, instead, self-criticism diminishes our self-respect and self-confidence and makes us far more likely to *repeat* our mistakes. By discarding such an unkind, even hostile attitude toward ourselves, we may be able to act differently on the next occasion; by maintaining it, we will not be in a position to learn much from bad experiences and will not improve.

Self-criticism and discouragement sometimes take the form of feelings of guilt. Guilt feelings are neither necessary nor helpful. We can make mistakes, even grave ones, without feeling "guilty" about it—which does not mean that we may not regret our errors and wish to make amends. To make a mistake is human and inevitable. Often the error results from an already restricted self-confidence, but, more frequently, it results from miscalculations that no one could have avoided making, for no one can ever know all the factors involved. The man who believes he "never makes a move until he has checked out all the facts" is either deluded or immobile; all "facts" are never available. The operation of unknown, extraneous variables confounds the calculations of scientists and schoolboys alike. In view of this, our "misfiguring" should make us feel at least as inferior as Albert Einstein when he made a mistake, but not more so.

Unfortunately, we can never be certain we are doing the right thing; only afterward can we know whether a decision was right or wrong. As it is, we are bound to do wrong on innumerable occasions. So what purpose is gained by feeling guilty? We cannot undo what has happened, and a person sure of himself will not waste his effort in crying over spilt milk. He will concentrate on doing his best in the resulting situation. A person who doubts his own ability and who, at the same time, must maintain his façade of good intentions will find it difficult to acquire this attitude of self-acceptance. Then guilt feelings come in handy. They seem to express good intentions despite a bad performance, and they justify our doubt about doing better hereafter. Guilt feelings divert our attention from what we *should* do to what we *have* done. They arise only when and if we are not willing to do what the situation requires.

Sometimes we suddenly feel the sting of guilt for what we may have done long ago. This concern with the past can arise only because the present confronts us with tasks that we want to avoid or for which we feel inadequate. Guilt feelings are an expression of discouragement and a justification for continuing and even intensifying our low opinion of ourselves.

If we recognize the trick we play on ourselves, we will not permit ourselves the luxury of guilt feelings. Instead of considering guilt feelings a sign of our high moral standards, as we are inclined to do, we should recognize them, with Nietzsche, as "indecent." We can be sure that as soon as we feel guilty, we are up to some new mischief. Such recognition can stop the vicious cycle of self-criticism and new mistakes, which usually follow each other in endless succession.

What should we do when we have made a mistake or done wrong? That is the time when self-encouragement is imperative. We can move toward amendment if this is possible; if not, we can take the incident and its consequences in stride as an inevitable part of life. If we were not preoccupied with our own value or the lack of it, we would not be much concerned whether a predicament arose because of our fault or because of someone else's. Most of us cope quite successfully with situations created by the blunders of others; for then we are task-oriented, not vanity-oriented. But when we fall in a stew of our own concoction, the first thing we do is turn up the heat. We flush with embarrassment, burn with shame, get red with rage at the culprit who "must" have pushed us in, or just sit and simmer in self-recrimination. To be able to make mistakes gracefully without shame or humiliation is an indispensable requirement for living. We must refuse to minimize our transgressions and look for scapegoats, either around us or within ourselves. Only then will we be able to do without some special success to "make up for" our failures. With the *courage to be imperfect* we can simply go on living, working, and functioning.

COURAGE

The product of self-encouragement is courage, the most vital quality in living. Courage alone permits the full utilization of our inner resources, in any given situation and for any given task. If we do not waste energy in proving our own worth, we can devote ourselves to useful objectives. If we do not anticipate failure, we can judge each situation adequately and act according to its needs.

Courage is the embodiment of self-confidence. It stems from faith in our own ability. It is a natural quality in all beings, as long as fear has not paralyzed them, but it is different from audacity and daredeviltry, with which it is often confounded. Courage is intrinsically correlated with a sense of responsibility, of belonging, because it reflects confidence in our ability to cope with whatever life may have in store for us. Courage is the opposite of fear, which is at the root of all evil. Courage permits proper judgment and, therefore, leads to effectiveness. It permits the full use of our physical strength, intellectual powers, emotional stamina, and creative imagination. It induces us to live in peace with ourselves and with others, since we are no longer afraid of others or of ourselves.

We question the possibility of living in peace with ourselves and others in a world that knows no peace. It seems impossible, but it is not. Our inner peace does not depend on the contingencies of life around us. Mankind has lost its paradise, if it ever had one. Life is always full of conflict, hardships, and predicaments. But a courageous person feels that he belongs to this life, is sure of his place in it, can look at it as a medium in which he lives, acts, produces, participates, and creates. He does not need a paradise; he finds satisfaction in his own fulfillment, in his own contribution and usefulness. He, too, may suffer accidents, disease, and tragedies. But his spirit remains unbroken; for there is always something to be done, some task in which he may enjoy the strength that life has bestowed on him. And there are always things to enjoy *if* one is willing to see them. This world belongs to the one who accepts himself as an integral part of it. In living, *we* are life.

Two apparently contradictory stories may emphasize the significance of such courage, and the various forms in which it can be expressed and experienced. First, there is the fable of the frog who drowned in cream because, having fallen in, he despaired of getting out; whereas his fellow frog, who kicked lustily against his fate, was able to leap to safety on the *butter* he had churned.

This is only a fable, however wise. The following story is

true. The Danube around Vienna is beautiful and warm in the summertime. The stream flows through lovely hills and villages, and a good many Viennese residents go upstream and swim down, carried by the water through the pleasant countryside. But every year several people drown, for the stream sometimes forms whirlpools. All these accidents could be avoided if people only knew that all they need to do in a whirlpool is to hold their breaths while the water pulls them down; in a few seconds the water will spill them out again. Instead, the unfortunate swimmers struggle against the current until they lose their strength and drown.

The moral of these two stories is simple enough. We must have faith in ourselves and in life. Then we can distinguish what is best to do in a given situation. Under certain circumstances we must act and not give up; under others, we must wait for our chance. Yet fear and resentment drive us to do the opposite: we struggle when we should wait and are laggard when we should move.

The wisdom of living is perhaps best expressed in a prayer that is widely known because Alcoholics Anonymous adopted it as its motto:

> God grant me the serenity
> To accept things I cannot change,
> Courage to change things I can,
> And wisdom to know the difference.

If we do not waste our energy trying to do what cannot be done, if we do not fight against facts of life that cannot be transformed, if we are willing to put up with the inevitable, we become free to use our energy to do what *can* be done, which usually is much more than we are inclined to assume. By not being preoccupied with our resentment of the conditions in which we find ourselves, we can spot the areas where change and improvement are possible. Our inner freedom is restricted by chains that exist only in our minds—by limitations that we impose on ourselves—because we cannot perceive the door that leads us out of our imaginary prison. We have become free, politically, through the democratic evolution, but we have not freed ourselves from the shackles of an autocratic tradition. We are, indeed, free men with slave mentalities, because we cannot visualize the freedom that we actually possess, even though we do not use it.

There are no rules, no absolutes to lend us the illusion of safety, but in our freedom to choose the way to go, we always have a chance. We cannot go against the stream, but the stream of life, of evolution, is with us. All we have to do is to swim with it.

THE STRUGGLE FOR PRESTIGE

In our culture prestige is the Golden Calf. At one time this calf was really "golden": money determined prestige. But whether we think of prestige in terms of money, or power, or talent and accomplishment, or any other form of success—prestige is still the Golden Calf of which we read in the Bible: a false god, substituted for what is really important in life, namely, to participate in social progress through useful contributions. We can find no satisfaction in being useful as long as we labor under the necessity of elevating ourselves above others, of achieving "success." When we strive for success, *whatever* we achieve is not sufficient; for our inferiority feelings linger and drive us on, *ad infinitum*. Many people who are considered highly successful flock to the offices of psychiatrists, who often are the only other people to know how these magnates and tycoons feel inwardly, how afraid they are of slipping, of not maintaining the high social status that they have acquired literally with blood, sweat, and tears. Getting old becomes unbearable to a man who has to be *first* in order to be *anyone* at all. Such people cannot content themselves to sit aside, to sip their wine and watch the dancers. To do that, as they see it, they would first have to step "down," from "above" their fellow men, and that would make them feel utterly worthless.

The desire for self-elevation and the pursuit of destructive compensations when status is threatened or denied lead to a universal demoralization. Corruption, selfishness, and abuse of man by his fellows are not new, but today there seem to be no limits to the urge to get ahead. Anyone struggling against vested interests and deploring the unfair treatment he receives tends to perpetuate the same behavior when *he* becomes a member of the dominant group. And neither the winner nor the loser in this struggle for superiority can feel secure; all are afraid, worried, anxious. Those who become discouraged in the competitive struggle for social superiority withdraw into useless forms of "achievement." The criminal "graduates" from a lower jail, climbing up the criminal social ladder to more serious crimes until he succeeds in attaining the "aristocracy" of the lifer. Dope addiction spreads as the embodiment of the mad drive toward easy pleasure and self-indulgence. Sex becomes heroic, a prime objective for pleasure and conquest.

Unless we realize our folly, we cannot do anything about it. Necessarily preceding any effort toward change and improvement is the conviction that we cannot obtain peace the way we are going. Yet it is almost impossible to convince anyone of the futility of striving for prestige and self-elevation, even when he is utterly miserable. The downcast man recites the strivings and "success" of others. He does not know how much they, too, pay for their drive, and he cannot see how miserable even the "successful ones" are: they are terrified of what would happen to them if they ever stopped their mad rush after prestige. Few realize that each of us already *has* a place in the world and could find satisfaction right where he is, without becoming more than he is.

Before we can abandon the struggle to gain prestige, we

need to examine another issue. The force of social conventions is strong indeed. Can we, by ourselves and for ourselves, defy the values of the community without becoming antisocial, without inviting ostracism and humiliation?

The answer to the above question is that we can and must. For the sake of the democracy that we have espoused, each of us must oppose the traditional tendency to pitch man against man. This is possible today, now that the time of expanding individual advantages, of "free-for-all" living, where each man had to look out for himself, has more or less passed. New social concepts are emerging and are gradually being incorporated into our general attitudes. A man who seeks only his own glory and pursues only his own interests may still be admired for his achievements, but we are beginning to appreciate even more the man who coordinates his personal interest with the public welfare and the interests of others.

Of course, we all are primarily concerned with our own advantage. But the way we seek fulfillment of our own needs distinguishes the egotist from the altruist. The egotist thinks he can serve his interests best by ignoring the interests of others, while the altruist realizes the advantage of bringing his interests in line with the interests of those around him. There is security in common interests and endeavors. There are two poles: security against or with others.

SECURITY IN CONFORMITY?

Concern with social integration and participation has brought about the modern trend toward conformity. The desire to belong has led to the submersion of the individual into the group. In looks, clothes, and behavior we try to be just like the others with whom we identify. In this way, we can be sure of our place, of a sense of belonging. Is this not the ideal of democratic participation among equals? Is this not a source of direction for the individual who needs the approval and direction of others, either from those within his immediate circle or from those who "count"?

David Reisman attributes the development of the trend toward conformity to economic and social conditions. So does Erich Fromm, who describes and decries the compulsive conformity prevalent in our democracy, what he calls the "automatization" of man in modern society. Fromm blames this development on "the market concept of value," on the "marketing orientation."[4]

The issue is *not* an economic one, however. As the rugged individualism around the beginning of this century prevented recognition of one's fellow man as an equal, so does the more recent trend toward group conformity. In a process of polarization group is set against group, each group looking down on outsiders. The ensuing restriction of free expression is no longer due to an autocratic regime, but to the equally inhibitive and cruel pressure of the group, pressure that stifles the individual's freedom of opinion and action.

The undesirability of this dependence on conformity is obvious; conformity prevents man from being free. The origin of this dependence may be traced to many factors.

There is first the understandable reaction against the previous emphasis on accentuated individualism. The "we" has become more important than the "I." This in itself is a necessary step toward social integration, particularly—and most importantly—a step toward social and group responsibility. However, this desirable and necessary evolutionary process is stymied and perverted in our present stage of democratic evolution. The same deficiency originally prevented the United States from founding a true political democracy and carrying out successful economic planning. A functioning

---

4. David Riesman, Nathan Glazer, and Reuel Denny, *The Lonely Crowd* (New Haven: Yale University Press, 1950); Erich Fromm, *Escape from Freedom* (New York: Holt, Rinehart, Winston, 1941), and *Man for Himself* (New York: Holt, Rinehart, Winston, 1947).

democracy needs the establishment and observation of *social equality,* which so far has been lacking. It is this lack that has perverted social adjustment and prevented effective political democracy, at least until now.

Yet it seems likely that this lack of individuality and freedom is not the *consequence* but the very *cause* of conformity. The trend toward full social integration and participation cannot come to fruition unless every individual is recognized as being of equal status. Man cannot be free to be himself, and therefore different from all others, as long as his social status is uncertain. Only social equality can provide this right and the opportunity for every man to be himself.

The flight into conformity is not an escape from loneliness, as Erich Fromm assumes, but a mistaken idea about finding a place. It is the fear of not belonging that prompts many people to accentuate their similarity to those with whom they wish to identify or who seem to be prominent—who therefore can guarantee status.

Submission to the group provides a false security because it neglects the most fundamental requirement of free man— his freedom of choice, his independence in thought and action. The individual cannot fulfill himself, he cannot play his part in life, if his "adjustment" consists of mere submission to an authority, to public opinion, or to a group. Adjustment to the status quo, submission to the existing social mores and values, is no longer possible. In times past, when social mobility was limited and evolution slow, this form of "adjustment" was the only one possible. Today, society is in flux, evolution rapid, and established norms no longer bind free men, who have the right and the duty to evaluate, to choose, and to change conditions. Adjustment today involves more than acceptance of the status quo; it implies the responsibility to stimulate change, to move with the group toward improvement. Each man's idea of society, of mankind and its future, is a moving force in the community. Conformity only to group conventions and standards neglects the individual's responsibility. The status that conformity provides is shallow and temporary, since the individual in a mobile society moves from group to group, being exposed to a variety of group pressures, choosing and rejecting one group after the other as he proceeds through life.

What other way to security is possible, then? Some people seek security through money or power; others through love or faith in God. All of these provide security in varying degrees, for each, within certain limits and as long as it lasts, secures a place for the individual. The benefit derived from money, power, and prestige is obvious; it is the social status they confer. People who hope to find security in love often place a great importance on the need to satisfy their emotional and sexual desires. They suppose that a sense of security is possible only if all their needs are met in a close and intimate relationship between two people.[5]

Yet many who have money, power, prestige, or love still are haunted by insecurity. How is this possible, since those assets provide status? The fallacy common to all of these people is the assumption that we can gain security from without, through something that is given or acquired. As long as our inner security depends on anything outside ourselves, we must continue to be afraid that we shall either have too little or lose what we have. Under such conditions security is an illusion. Those who make financial security their prime objective will not feel secure even with the greatest accumulation of possessions. They still may be apprehensive about

---

5. The prototype of the notion of "security through love" is the assumption that young children need love to feel secure. It is true that children need affection and warmth, but does that provide them with a sense of security? Not at all. Children may be very much loved and still be dissatisfied and rebellious. A mother's love does not always prevent her children from defeating her best intentions. Spoiled children will demand more and more signs of love in the form of indulgence so that they can do what they want.

their power or prestige in areas where money alone does not matter. Even the very rich may feel threatened, and those with great power and prestige often lack inner security.

Quite different are the effects of faith in God. It has no limitations. There is no danger of ever losing God's surveillance. Deeply religious people enjoy a strong sense of security. Nothing can really disturb their sense of unity with life. Even death is no threat. Whatever happens to them, it is the will of God, the result of His wisdom. However, for those who cannot accept the existence of supernatural powers, the important question arises: Is there a workable substitute for this comforting belief in Divine Providence?

The person who sincerely worships his God in whatever religious form derives his security not from God but from his own belief. It does not make any difference whether God actually exists; for the believer He exists because he believes in Him. It is *man* who determines the existence of God, His Will, Wisdom, and Providence. If the individual can find his security through his own thought and belief in God, then the source of his security *lies within himself.* He is able to create convictions that provide him with a sense of security, or with doubts that prevent it. The term most widely used to describe an attitude that produces a sense of security is "faith." Faith is considered characteristic of deep religious devotion. The question then remains: In whom can we have faith?

This is no problem for those who have faith in God or in His representatives on earth. But what faith can the others have? It seems self-evident that the era of democracy, of equality, demands faith in *man.* Without it there can be no democracy, no equality. But who—or what—is man? It is we— each one of us, you and I. If we have no faith in ourselves, we cannot have it in anyone else. We can have no faith at all. Faith in ourselves is the essential commandment of our era.

And what kind of man is it, in whom we have faith? Obviously only one who fully believes in himself. What is he like? He is sure of his place in the community because he is convinced, despite all his shortcomings and frailties, of his own value; he neither doubts it nor has to prove it. He has the realization of his own strength; therefore, whatever comes his way he can take in stride. He is not afraid of losing out because he does not worry about his prestige. All contingencies of life appear to him as challenges, as opportunities to use his brain, his muscles, his inner resources. The word "failure" does not frighten him. He may find a better or a worse answer to every challenge, but he will always try to do his best. He will do so not to "prove" himself but to survive, to function, to be useful, to fulfill his life. This is the only basis for a sense of security, the belief in ourselves, in our own strengths and abilities to deal as well as possible with whatever comes along —to take in our stride whatever may come. That is not selfishness because faith in ourselves permits us to participate, to contribute, to be useful to others.

Part II

PRINCIPLES OF MENTAL AND EMOTIONAL FUNCTIONING

CHAPTER 3 · **The Orchestration of Emotion, Mind, and Body**

So far we have described the predicament of modern man, the confusion in which he lives, and his futile efforts to find a place for himself. In this chapter we will try to analyze the psychological mechanisms that help us to understand man, his emotions and actions, and his attitudes to and relations with his fellow men.

THE FUNCTION OF CONSCIOUSNESS AND MEMORY

We have previously discussed the limitations of knowing oneself. We may find it difficult to convey to others a true picture of what we think, how we feel, what we believe. There is so much that goes on in us of which we are unaware.

The demarcation between what we know and what we do not know is not very definite. Adler maintained that there is hardly anything in us that we do not know at all, and nothing that we know fully. What we know about ourselves shows varying degrees of awareness. There is a continuum from the known to the unknown within each of us. We operate on a psychological economy principle: we know of ourselves only what we need or want to know. What we do not need to know for our functioning, or what we do not like to know, remains totally or partially unknown. We may even prefer not to admit to ourselves that we have decided what to know and what not to know.

The eye is a good illustration of this shading of awareness. The retina receives visual impressions, but only a small central part of the retina can give us clear pictures of objects, in regard both to shape and to color. The further away from the center, the more vague are the impressions. We need a wide field of vision to keep us informed about what is going on around us; if something becomes interesting, important, or threatening, we focus our eyes on the object, using the small area that permits clear vision. We can compare this center with conscious perception, and the rest of the vague impressions with the various degrees of awareness. Just as we see more than we realize, we know more than we can put into words.

Whereas our ability to know almost everything about ourselves is theoretically unlimited, we do not want or need to know everything. For instance, all the experiences we have ever had are imprinted in our memories. Under hypnosis, they can be recollected. But if all imprints were constantly in our consciousness, we would not only be overburdened but could scarcely pay any attention to present experiences. Consequently, the memory is so organized that we can take out of its "files" only what we need for the moment. We remember a name, a date, an event while it is useful to us. If we need it no longer, it drops into oblivion until we call it up again.

The function of the memory is only perplexing when it seems to defy our conscious intentions. Sometimes we try in vain to remember something. The imprint has always been there, as we discover when we suddenly remember, perhaps too late. Conversely, some thoughts seize upon us, and we cannot put them out of our minds, regardless of how we may try to "forget."

Is, then, the memory suddenly an independent organ over which we have no control? What in us stops or stimulates it at the "wrong" time and in the "wrong" way? Our memories are always at our disposal; they do only what we want them to do. But sometimes we are unaware of what we demand of our memories; or, rather, we do not admit to ourselves for what purpose we forget or keep "remembering," apparently against our wills. To understand such inner conflicts, we need to consider the two levels on which we all operate.

COMMON SENSE AND PRIVATE LOGIC

As members of the human community we share certain concepts and convictions, values and conventions. Our consciences, which we develop in childhood, represent the rules and regulations we have accepted. The conscience enables us to distinguish between "right" and "wrong." The content of the conscience may differ among individuals, but most members of a social and cultural group share concepts of right and wrong—otherwise they could not get along with each other. And because we all want to have status in the group, want to be recognized as "good" members of it, we try to live up to our good intentions—that is, try to abide by the directives of our conscience.

But as we have seen, hardly anyone always does what he is supposed to do, or always refrains from doing what he should not do. How is this possible, if we all want to be good and believe in our good intentions? Adler explained this discrepancy by referring to "private logic." This private logic expresses our *real* intentions. Each of us has goals that he cannot reconcile with his conscience; yet we manage to pursue our goals *and* maintain our good intentions! It takes intelligence to do so, but we have that. The child may want to get special attention or to show his power; he may want to do many things he knows he should not do. In our culture, with its superficial moralizing, he soon finds it profitable to find a good excuse. As long as he can "excuse" his bad behavior, he does not incur the full wrath of his parents or other authority figures. Nothing infuriates them more than the open admission of bad intentions. When the child breaks a window to punish his parents, he can do so and still maintain that it was just an accident. And as the child incorporates the pre-scriptions of the parents into his conscience, he eventually uses such excuses to placate his conscience as he had learned to placate his parents.

Our personal and private goals are not always in line with our consciences, but our goals motivate us in all our actions. If we behave improperly, we try to "rationalize" our behavior as if we were not responsible for it. We know that we should study for examinations, but if we feel that there is no sense in studying since we will not excel, we develop headaches, find it difficult to concentrate, or create similar neurotic symptoms, which then "excuse" our not studying—and may afterward "explain" our poor showing.

We do not admit this private logic to ourselves. If we did, we would have to take full responsibility for our actions and could no longer maintain our pretense of good intentions. No-body wants to lose face. So we must hide *our real intentions* from our own consciousness. We have developed various means to maintain this dichotomy between what we think we want to do and what we actually are doing.

One of the strongest excuses whenever we do not want to take full responsibility for our actions is provided by our emo-tions, at least as we experience them. And since emotions are one of the main sources for our self-deceptions, they warrant more detailed discussion.

THE FUNCTION OF EMOTIONS

Emotions are an integral part of man. His personality comprises three areas of function that are interrelated and integrated into one whole, the individual: bodily processes, reason, and emotions. In whatever man is doing, all three functions are involved, although it may seem in any given instant that he is dominated by one to the exclusion of the others. While the functions of reason and of bodily processes are well understood, the function of the emotions is not. Fortified by certain so-called scientific pronouncements, many people have either no idea, or only the wrong idea, about the function of emotions.

Emotions are not held in high esteem today. Describing a person as being "emotional" is generally not considered complimentary. Emotions are more or less distrusted. They seem to be irrational, provoking unwarranted actions. They are difficult to "control"; they distort perception and lead to misinterpretations of reality. We witness a tendency to blame anti-social behavior on emotions. They are considered the "lower" part of human nature, in contrast to reason and intelligence, which are the "higher" functions. Emotions are held to degrade man; reason to exalt him.

How could such a universal picture develop, fallacious as it is? Human progress has been based primarily on man's intelligence. The underlying emotions that have generated the scientific and intellectual accomplishments of the past few centuries are little noticed. Reason has been a strong tool in man's struggle for his emancipation from the force of nature and from mystical powers that had previously been considered the masters of his fate. Rationalism opposed mysticism; science became the only trustworthy approach to the discovery of truth. Objectivity became good; subjectivity, evil.

The inability of man to live up to the high standards of intelligence and reason he sets finds strong "scientific" support in those schools of thought that describe man as being propelled by animalistic drives and urges. This new mysticism, clad in scientific language, degrades man when it assumes the existence of a cesspool within each individual, containing all the repressed urges and drives that cause hostile and destructive emotions that interfere with man's best intentions. If these assumptions were true, man could never gain full dignity, or become fully responsible for himself. Yet this pessimistic view finds much acceptance.

It would seem more compatible with the dignity of man to acknowledge that it is not the power of emotions that disturbs social functioning but rather man's failure to understand and to use them properly, not as excuses, but as his most important assets.

The function of emotions becomes evident when we try to imagine what a person would be like if he had none. His ability to think could provide him with much information and help him generalize therefrom. He could objectively determine the pros and cons of every action. But he could hardly take a definite stand, or act with force, with conviction, because complete objectivity is not conducive to forceful action. Forceful action requires a strong personal bias, a subordination of certain considerations in favor of others. A completely unemotional person would be cold, almost unhuman. He could not experience friendship and closeness. He could not want anything very much and could not go after it. In short, he would be highly ineffectual.

Emotions provide the power, the steam, so to speak, for our actions: the driving force without which we would be impotent. They come into play whenever we decide to be forceful. They enable us to stick to decisions, to take stands, to develop attitudes, to form convictions. They are the only basis for strong personal relationships based on common interests and desires. They permit us to appreciate and disregard, to accept and reject, to enjoy and dislike. In short, they make us human instead of mechanical, men instead of machines.

The benefits and purpose of emotions are fairly easy to recognize when they seem positive, constructive, and helpful; it is difficult to appreciate emotions when they disturb. Then they seem to hinder us in what we want to do, in what we feel obligated to do. Only in such situations do we experience emotions as apparently uncontrollable. Then we dissociate ourselves from them as if we were not responsible for their existence. For this reason we are only too prone to accept theories that regard emotions as irrational forces that overwhelm us. For the same reason that people once believed in the devil, some now believe in the Id and the Unconscious.

Emotions that disturb are not essentially different from those that are positive and constructive. They are not irrational; it is only that their rationale is not understood or accepted, especially by the individual himself. The person or group against whom they are directed, however, may have no difficulty in recognizing the hostile purpose of such emotions.

EMOTION AND REASON

It is customary to assume that there is a sharp division between intellect and emotion, as if our intelligence would show us one direction and our emotions would drive us in another. Actually, both are interrelated and integrated, serving the same goal in different ways. Bodily functions, reason, and emotions do not "affect" each other, as a mechanistic viewpoint suggests; they present different aspects of the same process. The *body* "adjusts" itself to the *emotional* pitch to which the individual may bring himself on the basis of a conscious or unconscious *reasoning* process. Every process in the individual shows concomitant movements in all three areas of bodily activity: physical, intellectual, and emotional. The unity of the personality is always preserved, for each individual is a holistic unit. Mind and body are inseparable; they are only parts of the whole individual, who can use all his functions for whatever goal he has set for himself. The "whole" individual uses his body and his mind as he sees fit, as he can use each one of his hands in a different way and still coordinate their movement for a common purpose. One cannot say that the arms move independently, or that one hand "affects" the other, although they oppose each other when they grasp an object. It is equally impossible to assume that mind and body function independently, or "affect" each other. The individual uses all of his functions, although he may not always be aware of what he is doing with them.

To regard reason and emotion as divergent is in itself a "rationalization," a self-deception brought on by a derogatory attitude toward emotions in general. We assume rational intentions that we actually do not have. A distinction between "emotional" and "intellectual" understanding is nothing but a fallacy, as a classic anedote shows:

Father takes a walk with Johnny. A dog comes running after them, barking loudly. Johnny runs away and hides himself behind a tree. Father calls, "Johnny, don't you know that barking dogs don't bite?" From his shelter Johnny shouts back, "I know it and you know it, but does the dog know it?"

This illustration is typical of the assumed difference between intellectual and emotional understanding. Johnny accepts his father's opinion, because he has no good argument against it, but he simply doesn't believe it. In other words, what we call emotional understanding is an expression of our *real* beliefs, our real convictions. Intellectual understanding implies a superficial agreement. This "knowledge" of what one *should* do is "common sense." "Private logic" is our real conviction of what we believe and want, and it is therefore the reason for what we do.

Private logic is by no means illogical, once we recognize it. If it appears illogical, it is only because we do not choose to know our own motivations, our true intentions and goals. Reasoning and intellectual considerations are not foreign to emotions. Rather they are at the root of our emotions. Consciousness, full awareness, is not required for thinking, but all thoughts, whether we are aware of them or not, arouse supportive emotions. By merely thinking about something we stir up emotions that disappear when we change the direction of our thought. Thought and emotion are always concomitants: one provides the direction, the other the force of our movements. Emotions are like the gas in a car. We could not drive without it, but we put it in and use it as we decide.

THE FACTORY OF EMOTIONS

Since we need emotions for whatever we intend to do forcibly, we have devices at our disposal to create those emotions that can carry us toward our self-determined goals. Each one of us, for example, has a variety of symbolic words that provoke emotions of one kind or another. The words may be trivial, but the overtones and associations that we have attached to them make them powerful influences in our lives. We use them like pushbuttons whenever we are interested in stimulating certain emotions in ourselves.

We have many other ways to "create" emotions, supporting whatever pursuit we plan. Dreams, for instance, serve this purpose. Adler called dreams the "factory of emotions." While sleeping, we use our private logic without any interference from either reality or the censorship of our conscience. We create our dreams in accordance with our private logic. While dreaming, we depict events and situations of our own choice in order to fortify our attitudes. In our dreams we prepare ourselves for the next day, for things to come. We take a stand on the problems that we anticipate. We do not realize that we "create" our dreams, although we cannot do so consciously, deliberately. Nevertheless, we are the masters, for no power outside ourselves makes us dream. (Even penetrating stimulations from the outside are used in dreams according to our interests and attitudes.)

We could learn to understand ourselves fully, in our private logic and our motivations, if we could understand our dreams. But this we cannot do by ourselves. Even a trained psychotherapist, well equipped to understand and interpret the dreams of his patients, is usually at a loss when he attempts to analyze his own dreams. And there are good reasons for this perplexing fact. Dreams would lose their effectiveness if we understood them, if we realized that we created them and for what purpose. The whole problem hinges on our need for a personal bias in life. If we recognized our bias as such, we could no longer maintain it. Therefore, we must deceive ourselves. Our dreams are means for such self-deception.

THE NEED FOR SUBJECTIVITY

Subjectivity—the basis of our attitudes, emotions, and beliefs—is necessary for living. Without it, we could not function in the complexity of social life. We have to take a stand in line with our own interests, viewpoint, concepts. Without stands, each of us would be a machine without creative imagination and power. The very act of creativeness presupposes a bias, a personal preference or antipathy. We must be convinced of our own point of view, as opposed to that of others, and at the same time we must integrate all our biases for the common welfare, which depends on the synthesis of all opposing forces within society.

This is why no one can really know himself fully. We have to hide our subjective reasoning from our conscience and consciousness, otherwise we should weaken our position, our drive and effectiveness. But this lack of full knowledge need not be a threat. We may well one day be able to define clearly a "Psychological Uncertainty Principle," similar to the principle that Heisenberg established.[1] *We must get used to the idea that knowing everything is neither possible nor necessary.*

---

1. The Uncertainty Principle of Heisenberg states that one cannot know both the position and the speed of an electron. One knows for certain either one or the other, not both.

It seems that conscious knowledge about oneself is highly overrated; similarly, unconscious processes are falsely blamed for our deficiencies. Our individual strength is experienced without any interference by our conscious thoughts. Our consciousness is more often a handicap to our well-being and our functioning than impulses and motivations coming from the wide realm of the unknown in us. As a matter of fact, we can only function when we act as we are, whether or not we know what we are.

Correctly understood, our uncertainties are an asset: they give us not only the "right" but the opportunity to be subjective and biased. If we accept ourselves as we are, without rebellion or the need for so-called self-control, then we can utilize fully all our inner resources for whatever contributions we wish to make to the common welfare, to the progress of mankind.

THE LIMITATIONS OF SELF-KNOWLEDGE

We are now in a position to define more clearly what we cannot know about ourselves. Wherever our personal bias comes into play, we cannot, of course, be objective. We cannot "know" our bias, otherwise it would disappear, and along with it our distinctive personality. The first and fundamental bias is formed in childhood. Our impression of our position in the family and our interpretation of the early experiences to which we are exposed distinguish us from any other human being. These early impressions form the basis of our self-concept, of our *life style*. We are all living in the same world, but our individual concepts of this world vary. It is precisely this individual concept that makes each of us what he is. If we change our self-concepts, we become different. But none of us can change our self-concepts by ourselves.

The restrictions of self-knowledge are not limited to the basic self-concepts of our life style. Many of our motivations

as well must be hidden from our consciousness because otherwise we could not maintain them. *We never can be sure of
our motivations.* Again, this restriction can be regarded as a
strength and not as a weakness in human nature. Because of
the subjective ñature of our motivations, we have a right to
act without questioning constantly the "justification" of our
impulses. We have to accept our impulses as part of ourselves
and of our intentions. We need the courage to take full responsibility for our actions, although we may never know accurately the reasons for them. Then we do not need the self-
effacing fight with ourselves in which we subside into utter
incompetence. By abandoning the futile inner conflict, we
gain the peace of mind all seek and so few find.

It is not impossible, however, to reconsider our personal
biases and to do something about them, should they become
detrimental and disturbing. But this procedure requires outside aid, the advice of a technician who can examine the basic
dynamics of our biases and promote a change in them. Only
by means of such a process, presently called counseling or
psychotherapy, can we obtain insight into our basic concepts
and resultant motivations. In other words, only during counseling or psychotherapy, which is a process of relearning about
ourselves, can a limited insight and penetration of our biases
be accomplished. Only when an outsider provides more objective points of reference can an attempt be made toward an
objective evaluation of our inner dynamics and motivations.

But even after certain detrimental aspects of our biases
have been eliminated and we have acquired other and more
suitable biases, we continue with these new biases with the
same ignorance of our motivations.

Despite the limitations in self-knowledge, certain avenues
are open to us for gaining some insight, even without the aid
of psychotherapy. *Introspection* must remain vague and uncertain, but *observation* of ourselves can be highly beneficial.
We can—so to speak—look over our own shoulders at what

we are doing. Such an attitude of observation is the only effective approach toward some kind of self-understanding. We can focus only on our *actions,* not on what lies behind them. *We can determine the direction of our actions and draw some conclusions as to their purpose.*

THE MEANING OF OUR ACTIONS

The motivations of our actions are, as we have said, obscure, but the direction of our actions is generally obvious. We may not know the purpose of what we do, but we can see the results. If we are willing to put aside our rationalizations, we may discover a completely new perspective in evaluating ourselves, applying a principle that we all use, often unconsciously, for the evaluation of others. We judge others by their *deeds,* not by their *words.* If someone tells us how much he likes us, but treats us in an unfriendly fashion, he does not impress us with his friendship. We think that his actions reveal his true motivation more accurately than do his words.

In evaluating ourselves we generally adopt the opposite approach. If our actions are objectionable, we may point to our motives: we did not mean what we said or did; it was all a mistake or an accident. In other words, we discredit our actions and uphold our intentions. Thus we deceive ourselves.

The first step toward a better self-evaluation is to recognize our own pretenses. What we *meant* to do does not matter; what we *have done* is all that counts. By taking our actions at their face value, we may become willing to accept our full responsibilities instead of hiding behind our good intentions. Once we have accepted our actions as true expressions of our intentions, we can learn a good deal about ourselves. Watching our actions and their results, we can see whether they lead to cooperation or to friction; whether they contribute to the common welfare or do harm to others; whether they are directed *toward* others or *against* and *away* from them; whether

they stimulate closeness or distance. These are the fundamental objectives of everything we do, indicating the social
meaning of our actions and thereby reflecting our own social
attitudes. When we learn to perceive our actions, we can
change them—and through them, ourselves.

The term "action" should be understood in a broad sense.
Anything we do is an action, not only acts involving the use
of muscles. Even thoughts are actions. We do something and
move in some direction merely by thinking. Our thinking
gives us a good opportunity to recognize our intentions.

*It is sometimes assumed that thoughts are merely a prep-
aration for actions, but thinking can also be used as a substitute for action.* The thoughts that lead to actions differ characteristically from the thoughts through which we avoid
actions. Preparatory thinking is directive and progressive.
We consider the premises and draw our conclusions. Quite
different is the thought process that serves as a *substitute* for
doing. We may pretend to seek a solution while our thinking
prohibits arriving at any conclusions. Our thinking goes
around in circles; it is repetitious and stationary. The same
pros and cons are considered time and again, without
resolution.

Whenever we observe ourselves considering the same premises time and again, we can be sure that we are involved in a
process of self-deception. We are only pretending to find a
solution, while actually avoiding any action. Behind our
seeming overeagerness to reach a conclusion, we conceal our
unwillingness to move; we think "so hard" that we never stop
thinking and start acting. It is possible to "spot" such thought
patterns and thereby stop a pretense that, by its nature, can
lead to no good.

A related and frequent form of self-deception is indecision.
Here, too, we find an abundance of thinking without any
movement toward action. In contrast to the professed desire
to move, the actual behavior does not indicate any such in-

tention. Indecision is always self-deception, because it presupposes a conscious desire to do something when the prevailing desire is actually the opposite. Under the *pretense* of being *unable* to decide we *decide* to do *nothing*.

Take the example of the girl who cannot decide whether or not to marry a suitor. Although she does not know the purpose of her behavior, her indecisiveness makes it possible for her to shirk responsibility for whatever may happen. It prepares an excuse for all possible developments. If she is "swayed" eventually to consent to marriage, then she can always remember that she did not want to marry her man in the first place, and therefore has no obligation to make the best of it. And if the suitor, discouraged by her hesitation, finally leaves her, she can always blame him if she remains unmarried.

Yet the actual dynamics of the girl's behavior are even more interesting. One can prove to the girl that she has already made up her mind, and that she merely does not want to admit it to herself. If asked whether she thinks she will marry the man, she will undoubtedly give the expected answer, "I don't know." Does she visualize, that—let us say—a year from now she will be married to him or not? Which is more probable? In keeping with her assumption that she is undecided, she will naturally try to evade the question by saying that she simply does not know. But there is the law of probability: we do not know anything about the next moment, but we can take a certain outcome for granted because of its probability. If we ask her whether she will come home safely after she leaves the office, she does not "know," but she assumes that she will get home all right. She cannot be certain, but she still can rely on a high degree of probability. The same holds true for her possible marriage. Can she more easily imagine that a year from now she will be married to her present suitor? Or is it easier for her to assume that she will not be married to him by then? If she is not too reluctant to take on responsibility for her action, she will realize at this point that one or the other possibility is slightly easier for her to imagine. Whichever alternative is more probable, be the difference only 51 to 49 percent, indicates her present "decision." Whatever possibility she can more easily imagine reflects her present "intention." She may change her mind, of course, but as of today she has made it up, although in such a way that she can pretend to be innocent of whatever may happen because she has not "planned" it. Actually, her plan of action is ready, but she has tried to conceal it.

Another way of veiling the stands we take and the moves we make is the assumption that we stand still. Some really believe that they are inactive, that they do nothing. This is an obvious fallacy. As life moves on, nobody can stand still. Even trying to stand still is action directed *against* life, *against* participation. The flow of time is like an escalator; we are moving with it. The inevitability of movement belies the assumption of standing still. Whatever we do or do not do is an expression of our kind of participation.

Another concealment for our present attitude toward life is overconcern with the past and the future. The future, in particular, lends itself wonderfully to the pretense of meeting responsibilities that actually are shirked. The true significance of an overconcern with past and future is evident; it ignores the fact that we live only in the present moment. Our whole lives consist of sequences of moments. Only the given moment presents life, its obligations, and its necessities. Naturally, the present is embedded in the past and the future; it is the link between both. We can fruitfully think about the past to gain perspectives about the present, to apply lessons we have absorbed. And we can also think about the future to prepare our actions, to lay plans. Neither activity implies a preoccupation with the past or the future at the expense of the present. Yet this is exactly the purpose of preoccupations. The past and future appear more important than the trivialities of today—when present obligations are distasteful. Worrying about what the future may bring and what we will have to do *then* gives the impression of a high sense of responsibility and conceals our reluctance to take on the responsibility for today. *The only way to prepare for the future is to fulfill the demands of today. If what we have to do today appears too insignificant, then there is no chance of having anything better tomorrow;* for tomorrow will again be a trivial day, with all the duties and obligations that an overambitious person may consider beneath his dignity. Many use their professed idealism to reject their present obligations.

BEHIND OUR EMOTIONS

Actions and thoughts indicate the direction in which we are moving; through them we may discover some of the dynamics that operate within us. Similarly, emotions can serve as guides for insight, since they too have a goal and purpose and are directed toward or against somebody or something. We cannot fight against our emotions because they represent our actual selves, our real intentions. But we can learn to understand our emotions. Realizing the meaning and purpose of our emotions does not necessarily change them, but it can change them. If we reconsider our plans and our intentions, our emotions follow any new direction we may choose.

Of course, such self-observations should not become a daily diet. If self-observation becomes routine, it diverts our attention from the life problems we must face and solve; it makes us too self-centered and introspective and disturbs our well-being and our functioning. Moreover, self-observation may deaden the spontaneity of those very emotions that give our lives force and direction. Indeed, a *preoccupation with observing ourselves* may merely become another dodge, like the preoccupation with the past and the future. Any attempt to take stock of ourselves should be limited to a few proper occasions, when we are at a crossroad or realize a need to sit back and take inventory, to reconsider where we stand and where we are going. It is at times of crisis or when we feel cornered or at the end of our ropes—and such situations arise in anyone's life—that we may benefit from such considerations.

It would not be stretching reason too far to suggest that mankind itself is at such a crossroad today. The path of equality has already been chosen, but in many ways our concepts and attitudes are still based on traditional autocratic presuppositions. We need to redirect our goals, to draw new conclusions about our objectives. Massive introspection on a societywide scale is in order. With this end in mind it seems worthwhile here to examine some of the basic concepts and attitudes that are prevalent in our world today, making the transition to democracy a stormy and turbulent passage.

CHAPTER 4

**Interactions and
Interpersonal Relationships**

Certain attitudes and concepts are so fundamental that our whole lives—both personal and social—are characterized and determined by them. They either foster or prevent harmony and mutual cooperation. They are responsible for our success or failure, for the extent of our ability to live with each other.

BASIC ATTITUDES

Two basic groups of attitudes oppose one another, and each of these groups contains four attributes that supplement each other. The four constructive attitudes are the basis of cooperation; the four corresponding opposite attitudes are the source of conflict and friction. On one side are ranged social interest, confidence in others, sense of equality, and courage. On the other side are hostility, distrust and suspicion, inferiority feelings, and fear.

It may be helpful to recognize these basic attitudes in their relationship to each other, as pairs of opposites. Then they appear thus:

Social interest	Hostility
Confidence in others	Distrust and suspicion
Sense of equality	Inferiority feelings
Courage	Fear

These fundamental attitudes lead to certain behavior patterns, superficially designated as character traits. Hatred,

envy, jealousy, conceit, and deprecation of others are defense
mechanisms against the demands of life, employed to stifle
the natural human inclination toward participation in a social setting. Tolerance, kindness, and generosity, on the other
hand, express and strengthen the willingness to cooperate.

SOCIAL INTEREST

Social interest is the most important human quality. Social
interest is not innate. What is innate is our ability to develop
social interest. It is not static; during our lifetime we increase
or diminish it. When we are successful, we enlarge and intensify the area in which we feel a sense of belonging; when
we are unhappy or fail, we restrict it. All our failures express
a lack of social interest. Only where we feel a sense of belonging do we have a high tolerance level, so that we can take in
stride whatever life may have in store for us. The degree of
our social interest is constantly tested by all the adversities
that confront us throughout life. Outside the range of our
social interest, our fellow men appear as our enemies against
whom we have to be on guard. The ensuing feeling of hostility and suspicion prevents our cooperation.

Therefore, the feeling of belonging presupposes confidence
in others, who are perceived as fellow human beings in our
common task of service to the needs of all. If we cannot have
confidence in our fellows, our distrust and suspicion breaks
down our bond of common interests. The greatest source of
our distrust is due not to clashes of interest but to our concern
with status. Only if we are confident of our status as equals
can we be our brothers' keepers. Inferiority feelings under-
mine our courage and arouse fears, the chief obstacle to any
cooperation. For men who have become free and have discovered their equality to others, fear is sin, the attribute of slaves.
Our predisposition to fear is the remnant of a slave mentality
that we have not yet overcome.

Inferiority feelings and fear are the strongest deterrents to social functioning and to peace of mind. Without fear, and unaffected by a feeling of personal and social inadequacy, we can endure all the hardships of life and still be able to cooperate, to participate with others in common efforts, and to use our inner resources for the benefit of all. Inferiority feelings restrict the development of the all-important social interest; therefore, they can be regarded as the most destructive human characteristic.

INFERIORITY FEELINGS

We are dealing here with one of the crucial problems facing modern man. Man can function in a democratic era only as an equal among equals; he can do so only if he can extricate himself from the assumptions of individual inferiority that hold him enslaved, blind him to the realization of his strength, deprive him of his inner freedom, and of his peace and serenity. Inferiority feelings induce him to wage unnecessary wars, to be defensive against his fellow man, to strive for unreal or empty victories, instead of devoting his energies to making this earth a pleasant place for all men to inhabit. One of our main tasks in our effort to establish a stable social equilibrium in a democratic spirit is the elimination of individual and collective inferiority feelings to which we are conditioned, both by our inner constitution and by our traditions. No man can be free unless he frees himself from self-doubt.

The human race is receptive to a sense of inadequacy, first through the biological inadequacy of the human constitution (man's biological inferiority), and then through the realization of man's smallness and insignificance within the universe (man's cosmic inferiority). Conditioned to feel inferior by the vast odds that mankind has experienced in its struggle for survival, man is exposed to a personal feeling of social inferiority in a social organization that has not been based on equality for all. No social equilibrium is stable unless each member of the group is recognized in his equal social status, and social equality requires recognition by others as well as by the individual himself. Where such mutual recognition is missing, social struggle ensues. The struggle, in turn, deepens the sense of social inferiority in each antagonist. Children, particularly, bear the full brunt of man's failure to treat his fellow man in the spirit of equality. Freeing ourselves from our inferiority feelings is tantamount to extricating ourselves from cultural and social patterns presently surrounding us. But it can be done, and it will have to be done if we want to be free and to establish a truly democratic society.

The inferiority feeling is actually not an emotion that is "felt." The emotional aspect is only the outward expression; underneath is a *concept,* a belief, a reasoning process. We assume that we are, or may be, inferior to others, inferior to what we want to be or to what we think we should be. Although none of us can be perfect, or is ever as strong, able, or good as he could be, this fact in itself does not justify a feeling of inadequacy or inferiority. As a matter of fact, *the degree and intensity of inferiority feelings are in no way correlated with actual abilities or deficiencies.* It is not true that less capable and more deficient persons show stronger feelings of inferiority. Almost the reverse is true. The more ambitious a person is, the more accomplished, the greater his sense of inadequacy if he fails to obtain what he considers essential. Intense inferiority feelings are often found in those who, in the view of their contemporaries, have accomplished the most. This is an important fact. It invalidates the assumption that inferiority feelings are sometimes justified. The "superior" can feel inferior, and the less capable person can be free of any feeling of inadequacy. Therefore, *feeling* inferior to others has nothing to do with *being* inferior. We are dealing here with a subjective evaluation, a misappraisal of facts, based on a biased attitude toward oneself.

INFERIORITY COMPLEX

The high price we pay for our inferiority feelings is not always limited to general tension and anxiety, uncertainty, and insecurity. Doubt in our value may become so pervasive that compensation may be impossible. Then we declare bankruptcy, either within a particular field of activity or altogether. We give up and devote ourselves to the arrangement of excuses. Withdrawal from life and some or all of its tasks is the only alternative. While the inferiority feeling stimulates compensatory efforts of one kind or the other, the inferiority complex, the deep conviction of a final deficiency, no longer permits any such compensation. If sufficiently discouraged, both children and adults make themselves appear weaker and more deficient than they really are. Neither coaxing nor persuasion has any effect. They hide themselves, so to say, behind real or imagined deficiencies in order to avoid any task that will make their deficiency become painfully obvious—and perhaps even more embarrassing. They prefer to declare themselves failures *before* they are tested. Some people may exhibit such an attitude only in work, or in sexual relations, or in social contacts; in unaffected areas they may still be able to function because they trust their abilities there. Others, however, give up entirely. Our mental institutions, jails, and flophouses are repositories for those who have given up hope that anything they can do will provide them with social status.

The crucial question is: Do the deviant, the failures, first have to overcome their deficiency before we can treat them with respect, or do we first have to treat them with respect before they can be rehabilitated? The following example highlights a very sad chapter in our present dealings with all those unfortunates who are sick or deficient. The story was told by Dr. Frieda Fromm-Reichmann in an address at a meeting of the American Psychiatric Association.

Dr. Fromm-Reichmann, the director of a sanitarium, was closing her office after a difficult day, when a young girl, a schizophrenic patient, came to talk to her. In one way or the other the girl provoked her, and Dr. Fromm-Reichmann became very angry. Of course, Dr. Fromm-Reichmann, a very sensitive and sympathetic person, almost at once became very distressed. She regretted deeply what she had done; she should not treat a *normal* person like that, to say nothing about a sick girl who was not responsible for what she was doing, she thought. But next morning, when she came to her office, she found in her mailbox a letter from the girl, thanking her profusely for what she had done. She wrote, "It is a long time since somebody treated me like a normal human being."

There is a lesson we all can learn from this episode: treat everyone—patients, charges, all those who are in trouble— like human beings. They are much more like normal people than we assume. They merely have false ideas. Even the psychotic's delusions and hallucinations are like the dreams of the normal person. What distinguishes him is the fact that the schizophrenic dreams "with open eyes." Recent studies on dream-deprivation indicate that a person deprived of dreams for a period of days often begins to act like the psychotic, dreaming while awake.

MENTAL ILLNESS, A WAY OUT

Traditionally, we have come to accept three main forms of psychopathology: neuroses, psychoses, and what previously has been called psychopathic personality and is now "character disorder." Depending on the orientation of the therapist, the dynamics in each of the three so-called disorders are explained and understood in an entirely different way. Szasz[2] denies that there is any mental illness; others regard almost every deviation from proper behavior and function as sickness, particularly if such deviations are found in children.

The increasing number of children who do not function properly are now called "emotionally disturbed." Yet often I find such children to be merely socially maladjusted, not emotionally sick. Thus we can consider the psychiatric specialty of child psychiatry a gross exaggeration. Generally, the "patients" the child psychiatrist sees need guidance and education, not therapy. Of course, there are mentally sick children, but they are the truly psychotic and form a relatively small group.

The tendency to look for organic factors to explain abnormal behavior depends on the political outlook of the observer. Thus it has been found that conservative and autocratic people look for hereditary or physical causes, while the liberal and democratically oriented emphasize psychological factors.[3] This has become a highly contested issue in regard to learning difficulties in children.

As I see it, all psychopathological conditions indicate an escape from social demands, with characteristic mechanisms in each form of disorder. Neurosis is merely a pretense of sickness, a subjective feeling of being sick, while psychosis is a condition of extreme malfunction occurring without the patient's realizing that he is sick. The nature of the response to conflicts distinguishes the types of psychiatric disorders.

The neurotic escapes his sense of failure by creating symptoms to excuse it. Symptoms always develop in a crisis situation in which a person cannot function on the basis of his life style. Each individual, therefore, has his own danger zone:

2. Thomas S. Szasz, *The Myth of Mental Illness* (New York: Harper & Row, 1961).
3. Nicholas Pastore, *The Nature-Nurture Controversy* (New York: King's Crown, 1949).

one gets sick when he can no longer work; another when he is no longer supported and has to begin to work. The mechanism of developing symptoms has already been discussed; we can actually "choose" any symptom we want if we begin to fight with ourselves. In a crisis situation innumerable opportunities appear for such a fight with ourselves. Symptoms are chosen according to their effectiveness: when one symptom does not bring the desired results, another is developed.

The vast majority of our contemporaries are neurotic because each finds himself in an area in which he does not believe in his ability to succeed or to master a predicament. *His neurosis is a facsimile of a disease.* A sickness is characterized by two factors: inability to function and discomfort. Because the neurotic—like all of us—is inclined to suffer, we all are susceptible to the sensation of being sick, particularly when the discomfort from the pain and the suffering leads to a disturbed function. But, simply put, neurotic symptoms help a patient to save face for not doing what he knows he should do.

The problem is quite different in psychosis, particularly in schizophrenia. Here the patient is so overwhelmed with his feeling of deficiency and his total lack of social interest that he withdraws from reality and creates, through his delusions and hallucinations, his own world in line with his private logic. When we reach such a patient so that he feels "understood" and "belonging," the schizophrenic process is arrested.

So-called character disorders assume great prominence on the contemporary scene. A person who loses faith in his ability to succeed within society can easily "succeed" by violating and disregarding society's demands. He suddenly changes from an inferior to a superior position. Most juvenile delinquents display an air of "moral superiority." They will admit that they are doing wrong, but they always succeed in blaming someone else or society as a whole for their wrongdoing. Contempt for and disregard of social demands are equally disturbing to society whether people act through idealism or through deviation. Opposition to existing social demands can lead to progress or to anarchy. The reformer may be regarded as a criminal if he fails or as a hero if he succeeds. And who knows which will happen? In our state of anarchy, of anomie, lack of order and of values, a state of general warfare has developed. The delinquent and the criminal provide the prototype of anti-social "success." Since they do not share the values established by society, they live by their own standards.

Part III

DYNAMICS OF CONFLICTS:
FROM CHILDHOOD TO ADULTHOOD

Few people are aware of the predicament of our parents or of the pathological condition under which we are living. There probably has never been a living being on this earth who did not know how to bring up its young, except our generation of parents. They have not the slightest idea of what to do with their children. Most parents have the best intentions, but lack the means of carrying them out.

W. C. Kvaraceus speaks of the "continuum of norm-violating behavior" of our children. On one end of the continuum is the child whom you can't get up in the morning or get to bed at night, who eats too much or too little, does not take on responsibilities, fights with his brothers and sisters, does not do his homework or chores—in other words, the average child. On the other end of the continuum is the juvenile delinquent. There is no qualitative difference between them, only a quantitative difference, that is, the degree of rebellion against order and against the demands of adults.[1]

How did this state of affairs come about? Kvaraceus attributes it to the intrusion of low-class morality into middle- and upper-class families, but a hundred different explanations are given for the inability of our parents to influence children.

Raising children has always been a matter of tradition. Parents have not needed lectures, books, and counseling in order to know what to do with their children. They have been

---

1. W. C. Kvaraceus, *Delinquent Behavior* (Washington, D.C.: National Education Association, 1959).

guided by tradition, learning from one generation to the other. Thus when Margaret Mead observed primitive societies in the South Sea Islands, she noted that each tribe raised its children in a different way, bringing up different personality types.[2] But one may well imagine that in each tribe the children were treated in the same way for hundreds of generations, and every adult and child knew how to deal with each other.

Our dilemma is the consequence of the democratic evolution that reached its peak in the United States after World War II. An unheard of degree of equality imbued every person with a sense of his rights. Nobody was willing to accept the dictates of the previously dominant group. Women no longer bowed to the demands of their husbands. And when the husband lost his power over his wife, both lost their power over their children. Parents can no longer "make" a child do what he should or stop him from doing what he wants. The same situation has developed in the relationships between labor and management and between blacks and whites. The methods effective in an autocratic setting—primarily the pressure from without through reward and punishment—have become obsolete. And the methods of stimulating children from within are little known to parents and teachers.

One of the greatest handicaps parents face is their lack of information about democratic methods, the only methods applicable today in solving conflicts. Ignorance of such democratic procedures is as great within the family as outside it. Parents bear the full brunt of this cultural deficiency, for they recognize their obligation to keep order and harmony within the family but find that the traditional methods—the only ones they know—are altogether futile.

The deficiency of a mother to raise her children properly

2. Margaret Mead, *From the South Seas* (New York: William Morrow & Company, 1939).

cannot be blamed on the mother's personal maladjustment. It is the cultural pattern that prevents parents from being effective. No two mothers are alike in personality, background, and education, yet *all* mothers make the same mistakes. They talk too much and take on too much responsibility. They suffer from a cultural concept about the role of a "good mother." They take on all responsibility, and the children do as they please.

Before parents can hope to learn to apply new, adequate methods of influencing and guiding children, another even more disturbing element will have to be dealt with, the warfare existing between adults and children.[3] As long as the warfare continues, few individual parents will be able to extricate themselves from the contemporary cultural pattern and to apply methods, based on mutual understanding, trust, and respect, that tend in turn to promote such qualities.

THE WAR BETWEEN THE GENERATIONS

We are witnessing today a battle between the generations that is often open but more frequently under cover. This is by no means new in the history of mankind; the battle between generations is as old as the battle between the sexes. Whenever one group set itself up as superior, the subjugated group has always rebelled. In an authoritarian society, however, the group in power had social support so that the rebellion could seldom be openly expressed. Today, in contrast, when the society no longer necessarily sides with the group in power, our generation of embattled parents faces public accusation and incrimination.

---

3. Very few educators and child psychologists realize the significance of generalized warfare between all adults and all children. An exception is Maria Montessori, who, shortly before her death, made a touching appeal for "Disarmament in Education" (*Montessori* magazine, Vol. 4, 1950, pp. 9–27).

Yet, though many parents do not treat their children wisely, the fault is less theirs than that of the whole present adult society. The assumption that many parents reject their children and do not love them is, unjustified in most cases. They fight with them because they feel defeated by them. In such circumstances parents cannot show how much they love their children.

CHILDREN ARE EQUALS

It seems preposterous to most adults, particularly to parents, to consider children as equals. In our efforts to combat our feelings of inferiority we are constantly seeking reasons to justify our assumption of superiority over others. Where do we find better reasons than with our children? Children are small. "Big" and "small," like "strong" and "weak," are prototypes for an assumed scale of superiority and inferiority; persons that are small in size and limited in physical ability, skills, and experience are considered inferior. Even when we know that no lack of qualities or abilities deprives a person of his due respect, of his place in society, we maintain this fair attitude only as long as we are not threatened in our own status. But adults are constantly threatened by their children. Consequently, they compensate by emphasizing the child's smallness and weakness. Their difficulties arise from their inability to "control" their children, and thus they are unwilling to recognize the child as an equal and to treat him as such.

The child, at any age level, is a typical human being who wants his place in the group and rebels against being subdued. The ensuing struggle characterizes our present homes and educational institutions; many families, particularly those with young children, begin every day with a fight. As long as we remain emotionally and intellectually unprepared to recognize the child as an equal, we cannot guide him in a democratic atmosphere. The exhibition of our prejudice prevents the child from feeling that he belongs to our society, within the family and within the school as well as within the community. The child then behaves like a foreigner, an outsider, and in most cases he is treated as such. Few adults treat the child as they would another adult.

WHY WE MISTRUST OUR CHILDREN

Why do adults look down upon children and think they are entitled to feel superior to them? As in all cases of prejudice, we must look for some threat, some fear of inadequacy, that stimulates the desire of self-elevation. Such fears are easily detected among adults.

Parents and teachers seldom know how to influence children. They are aware of and accept their responsibility for raising, teaching, and influencing them, but since teachers and parents cling to traditional and ineffectual methods, children do not respond to their educational directives. In turn, adults feel frustrated and defeated, and a vicious cycle sets in. Driven by their sense of responsibility, adults cannot tolerate defeat. They become deeply afraid of the possibly tragic consequences that may ensue if they cannot control the child and compel submission, acceptance of their suggestions, and acquiescence to their requests for proper behavior. Parents and teachers are frequently unaware that they are acting not in the child's interest but in the interest of their own badly shattered authority. Then, as they increase their pressure to ensure obedience, the child increases his rebellion and defiance.

There are further reasons why adults mistrust children. Since adults themselves feel inadequate in a world full of danger, change, and insecurity, they assume, *a priori*, that a small, undeveloped child must be in even greater danger and feel even more insecure than they. Consequently, the child's obvious limitations of strength and skill seem to *justify* a lack of confidence in and respect for his ability. It appears to be unthinkable that the child can take care of himself and manage his own affairs. Moreover, father and mother, constantly fearful for their prestige in the outside world, look for a secure position for themselves at home with their children. There, at least, they can hope to be appreciated as big, strong, and capable. Parents, and particularly mothers, seek to prove their worth through their children. They may not realize how often they try to impress their children with their own abilities. And it is gratifying to do everything possible for a small, helpless being!

Often adults try to present themselves as shining examples. While the children are small, they may be impressed with the knowledge, strength, and ability of their parents. But soon parents find, to their dismay, that the children are not only unimpressed with, but actually challenge the parental superiority. It is even worse if the child continues to believe in the superior power of his father and mother; then his own development may be endangered. A son impressed with his father's masculine strength may doubt that he will ever be able to become a "real man." And the accomplished and efficient mother may ask herself in surprise why she deserves such a lazy, slow, and untidy child.

Self-indulgence, too, enters this struggle between parents and children. Most of us are more or less spoiled children. We have not learned to take things in our stride. We want our own way; otherwise we feel defeated. In our struggle with our children we quickly reach the limit of our endurance, which terminates our decent behavior. We may rationalize our self-indulgence by our interest in the child's welfare. We spank the child for *his* good—so we think. Actually, we cannot stand the child's defiance. Or we may yield to the child's undue demands because we do not want *him* to suffer when he cries. Actually, we are the ones who are suffering because we cannot stand his crying. In all such cases, parents are concerned more with their own feelings than with the welfare of the child. Their own discomfort evokes their hostile actions, which prevent them from being the child's real friends. They compete with the child as to who will have his own way. Each tries to win. All lose. In the meantime we are raising a generation of tyrants: children who intimidate and have learned to defeat us.

OUR MISCONCEPTIONS ABOUT CHILDREN

The prevalent concept of what children are confirms our assumption that adults are prejudiced. Certain scientific opinions, widely accepted because they fortify this prejudice, are based on the assumption of man's animal nature. The infant is viewed as a parasitical being, driven by animalistic urges, instincts, and drives; he tries selfishly to satisfy his instincts and must be "tamed" in the right way before he can become a truly social being. Most adults, not knowing that a child can behave sensibly and be trustworthy, treat him as if he were irresponsible. Even very young children have more sense than their parents are inclined to assume and, not too rarely, more than their parents have. Even infants respond to social demands voluntarily if they are properly treated—with respect and without indulgence. Children accept responsibility at a very early age if the adults give them the chance. They operate by trial and error, and that which gets them the desired results will be continued.

As to intelligence, not only do children have it, they also make excellent use of it. Of course, parents may not realize this because the child's goal may differ from theirs, and he may, therefore, use his intelligence against them, and not in line with what they want.

Although the child does not know why he is misbehaving, the trained observer can see that even the worst kind of behavior has a purpose.

We have observed *four goals* in child misbehavior. They express the child's mistaken assumption about being significant and having a place. The child may try to keep his parents busy with him (goal 1); to involve them in a power contest (goal 2); to hurt them as he feels hurt by them (goal 3); or to be excused from tasks where he expects to fail (goal 4). And while I will discuss these goals in greater detail later, it is enough now to say that the child is not aware of his intentions. But he responds with a "recognition reflex" when his goal is revealed to him.

Round after round, the child outsmarts his parents. The child's behavior is logical and intelligent, provided one knows how the situation appears to him. But to the parents, who fail to recognize the field of action in which they and the child are operating as social antagonists, the child's behavior may appear senseless or irresponsible.

A child is not a parasite, as many experts want us to believe. True, an infant cannot move on his own or find food by himself. In this sense he depends on his mother. But this is true also for the sick and the crippled, whom nobody insults with words such as "parasite" or "immature." Even an infant can take care of himself to a greater extent than most parents suppose. The limitations of his muscular strength, of his comprehension and intellectual facility do not make him "inferior" or fundamentally different from any other human being. Many deficiencies in children are artifacts, promoted by parents who are not aware of an infant's or young child's many abilities.[4] While the parents do not "cause" a child's defi-

---

4. The extent of an infant's ability to size up a situation and to cope with it effectively and intelligently has been demonstrated by normal infants of deaf-mute parents. They will cry without making any sound, since they realize its futility. A newborn infant born to deaf-mutes will cry with sound for one or two months and then give it up when it does not get him a response. When they are older, the children stamp with their feet if they get angry because the parents can perceive the vibration of the floor and respond.

ciency and misbehavior, they make them possible through their responses.

THE FALLACIOUS CONCEPT OF "MATURITY"

Whenever prejudice against a group becomes prevalent, some term is likely to be coined, symbolizing group antagonism. For example, so thoroughly have our children defeated and frustrated the adult generation that in revenge we have had to invent a fitting epithet. Characteristically, we hide our antagonism in an oblique attack. We do not speak derogatorily of the child as such; we call an adult who does not behave properly "immature." This epithet obviously implies a superiority in adults who are "mature." It also implies that an adult who is maladjusted is acting "childishly" and is therefore inferior. Yet there is no proof that maturation means achieving superiority. It merely suits the adult to think so.

The concept of maturity is one of the most dangerous fallacies afflicting our already sufficiently confused generations. Troubled people, especially children who are discouraged, are now disparaged and further discouraged by being labeled with the technical term "emotional immaturity," which means nothing to them and gives them neither understanding nor direction. The term provides only an additional excuse for not behaving properly, for the "immature" *is conditioned* to behave "immaturely"! In fact, an "immature" adult and a child have one thing in common: the difficulty "mature" adults experience with either type of person.

What is meant by "maturity"? Maturity connotes a sense of reality, proper perspective, unselfishness, control of emotions, reliability, and independence—in short, proper social and emotional behavior. There can be no doubt that many people lack some or all of these qualities. But the term "immaturity" *implies that such deficiency is normal for young children* and abnormal only for older youth or adults. Yet when children are uncontrolled, selfish, and do not behave properly, they are so because of faulty rearing—not "childishness." Eventually, too, faulty child behavior becomes faulty adult behavior. Adults who behave properly and are judged to be mature generally behaved in the same way when they were young. Proper behavior and social adjustment, maturity, have nothing to do with age or with the process of growing up.

Maturation can only imply a development through growth. In certain areas—as in physical development, glandular function, skills, and knowledge—such growth takes place as the person goes through infancy and childhood and becomes an adult. But in social and emotional adjustment, no such change occurs in the process of growing up. During puberty the child learns to mask his real intentions. Children are distinguishable from adults less by a lack of good qualities than by an abundance of them, too often lost in the process of growing up. Children who have not yet learned to cover up are much better able to express their intentions and attitudes; they are more sensitive to the nature of personal relations and to a given social atmosphere. They are usually creative and imaginative. All these "good" qualities in the growing child often are stifled by the contemporary methods of training. Adults often are less rich and resourceful than they were in their childhood, but—as compensation—they consider themselves mature and superior.

If we were not so prejudiced against our children, we should consider being called childish or infantile as praise, not as disparagement and humiliation. Anyone who knows how to deal with children will agree that children are much more responsive, much more sensible, ready, and quick to understand and to change than are adults. In child guidance counseling I find almost daily evidence of how much more quickly the child can comprehend his role within the family if it is explained to him, how much more rapidly he can grasp the significance of interpersonal dynamics, and how much more readily he can change, than can his parents.

Labeling someone "emotionally immature" and "childish" is nothing but name-calling, and the practice of name-calling is contagious. As soon as a label receives general acceptance, it is used whenever someone arouses our antagonism. But we should not forget that no supposedly infantile adult behaves as normal children or infants do. The concept of maturity is a means of self-glorification for an adult population that feels defeated by its children.

THE CONSEQUENCES OF OUR PREJUDICE

Many methods used in child-raising today reflect the mistaken picture that parents have of their children. Predominant is the tendency to overprotect them. Since there is actually no need for such treatment, it can stem only from the interests and motivations of the parents. It often is the desire of a mother to feel important and to prove her own value that impels her to consider her child helpless, unable to protect himself. She visualizes dangers to justify her inclination to remove obstacles from her child's path. Letting him experience his own strength and build up his resistance to dangers would deprive her of her own importance; overprotection deprives the child of both strength and self-reliance and keeps him dependent.

Similar dynamics operate when a parent spoils a child. Spoiling may imply overprotection, undue worship, overindulgence, undue service, but at the root of all spoiling lies the assumption that the child should enjoy his privileges now and will later learn to get along without them. But this "later" never arrives. Once the child has accepted special privileges, he holds onto them, and when the parents later try to "break him away," he feels abused and fights for the special status he enjoyed before. When the child is treated like a prince because he is "only a child" or a baby, he does not experience his equality, his being like others. He would be much happier if he were treated like anyone else. Spoiled children, as a rule, are unhappy children. They do not learn to rely on their own strength, which alone can provide a sense of security. They rely on others, gain their status through others, and become deeply convinced that by themselves they are nothing.

Some "experts" do not recognize the child as a human being but regard "it" as just a bundle of drives, something that selfishly seeks gratification and has to be cuddled and satisfied in order to become human. They assume a natural "dependency" in the child, which permits him to function and to feel secure only through his mother's love. We are told that such "dependency needs" have to be met; otherwise the child cannot become independent. Such "experts" consider deprivations of instinctual desires as the cause of all maladjustment and implore mothers not to frustrate their children by denying them gratification, even if such gratification disturbs order and places the child in a special category. Because the innate strength of a baby and his ability to adjust himself to social situations go unrecognized, they are not taken into account as a source of social functioning. Thus a mother who is advised to give in to the child in order to "satisfy his needs" often finds herself confronted with a child who takes advantage of her by increasing his demands, instead of becoming progressively more independent. Although the mother may for the moment avoid conflict and tension when she fulfills the child's demands, long-range peace and harmony cannot be achieved through indulgence and submission. The mere notion of a child's dependency needs is fallacious. The "dependent" child soon becomes independent when the mother stops being impressed with his real or pretended weakness.

A disobedient child is always a domineering child. By refusing to do as he is told, he forces his parents into actions they do not want to perform. In the crucial moment, when the child could learn from the consequence of a disturbed order, the parents feel sorry for him and try to "spare" him the predicament. *They* take on *his* responsibility, be it in regard to schoolwork, food intake, cleanliness, or order in general. Instead of minding their own business, they mind his. If the mother could only stand aside, in a friendly and patient manner, the child would lose his power over her and learn to respect the order for his own benefit.

The subtle distrust of the child's abilities that underlies parental spoiling is often concealed behind a mother's concern for the child's welfare. Few mothers can resist the temptation to exhibit their controlling wisdom. The child is told on innumerable occasions what to do and what not to do, although it should be obvious to any impartial observer that he already knows what to do because he has heard it often enough. Often parents expect their child to act in the worst possible way, and then their very anticipation tends to provoke him into doing what they expect, partly in defiance of them and partly in sheer acceptance of their low opinion of him. If parents only knew—and this is true for many teachers also—that telling a child repeatedly not to be so clumsy, stupid, selfish, or bad actually means telling him that they expect him to be so and induces him to prove them right! Distrust is poison to any relationship. Generally, a child trusts his parents no more than they trust him. Many children are convinced—and perhaps with good reason—that their parents understand them less and are less fair to them than any stranger would be.

Few parents realize how often they humiliate their children. Even tone of voice can indicate lack of respect. It is either cooing or complaining, "explaining," accusing, ordering, or threatening. On a playground or wherever mothers and children gather, we can see how few mothers can even talk to their children in a tone customary between normal people. Scolding and fault-finding are the daily routine in many families.

THE CHILD RECIPROCATES

At first, children are inclined to participate and to be helpful around the house, but their efforts are soon stifled by adults, fearful of the damage the child may do to objects or to himself. Whatever has to be done within the family is done by parents and older siblings; little is left for the small child. The development of a natural sense of responsibility and social interest is hampered; the child's usefulness is stifled by lack of opportunities for contributing to the welfare of others. Nothing of this kind is expected from a young child. All he can do for others is to be charming, cute, playful, precocious, entertaining—and unobtrusive, so as not to disturb any adults or cause them any discomfort. If we compare the performance of our young children with what children at a very early age are expected to do and can actually accomplish in other cultures, we recognize how great is the waste of ability and inner resources in our generation of children. And unfortunately this waste occurs during the most important period of life, when the basic concepts of ourselves and of life are formed. Then, after the child has been prevented from making contributions, he is confronted suddenly with demands, and these demands are supported by the challenge to "prove" his value. No child is permitted to feel good enough and adequate as he is. Only after he has grown further, learned more, increased his ability and knowledge, will he perhaps have a chance to think himself worthwhile. Many children are given the idea that excelling is the only basis for being good enough, and these early experiences in childhood contribute greatly to the deep feeling of social inferiority characteristic of our adult contemporaries.

The following example gives the lie to our misconception

about very young children. Once, in Europe, I took a hike through the hills around Vienna. It was hot, around noontime, and I wanted something cold to drink. I entered a farmhouse hoping to get some milk, but only three young children were present. I asked where their parents were and was told that they were out in the field working. "And who is taking care of you?" I said. The oldest child, a girl, said she was. When I questioned her further, she said that she dressed the other children, gave them lunch, and kept them busy until their parents returned. "And how old are you?" I asked. She said, "Four years."

When I told the above story to my students some thirty years ago, they expressed surprise at the girl's age, but a foreign guest, a professor of psychology from Switzerland, thought their reaction a most impressive expression of American attitudes toward children. He asked in surprise, "Don't you know what four-year-old children can do?"

Because we make it difficult for children to find their place in the family through useful contributions, they look for different means to gain a sense of significance. All their nonconformity and inadequate behavior is motivated to this end, to compensate for the low status in which they find themselves. Moreover, little is accomplished by labeling such misguided efforts as "bad." The label only increases the child's conviction that he is inferior, and this sense of inferiority, in turn, intensifies his compensatory warfare.

Our methods of raising children confront them with a series of discouraging experiences. And they themselves often use their smallness and assumed or real inability to hold their parents in their service. The child may begin to demand attention in a variety of ways. He seeks constant and repeated demonstrations of love, gifts, and services. If he does not satisfy his goal of attracting attention through useful means, through charm and smartness, then the child may switch to the useless side and misbehave. In one way or another the child is going to fulfill his primary goal, to gain attention (goal 1).

When parents try to put a stop to a child's undue demands for attention, a struggle for power evolves (goal 2). Children really believe that they have a right to do what they want, and that anyone who tries to stop them is being unfair and shows a lack of love. The contest for power between parents and children is becoming increasingly common. During the last few years, an alarming number of young children, primarily boys, have become veritable tyrants, intimidating their parents and defeating them. Tell them what to do, and they will refuse to do it; tell them what not to do, and they feel honor bound to do it. And few parents or teachers know how to cope with such a power-drunk child.

The average age of such domineering children seems to be decreasing as time goes on. Once it was primarily the adolescent group that became involved in such power contests; then there was an increase among members of the preadolescent group. A few years ago I was impressed with the large number of four- to six-year-old boys whose mothers were actually afraid of them, notwithstanding their own efforts to overpower the child. More recently children as young as one and a half have been found in this category, and girls have begun to enter their ranks. In short, warfare between the generations is growing more intense.

The parent-child power contest leads inevitably to a state of mutual retaliation. If the fight becomes violent, the child may be confronted with so much hostility, not without engendering it, that he feels disliked by everybody. Yet despite his conviction of ostracism, the child still does not give up his efforts to make a place for himself in the group. But since there is no constructive way left open for him to achieve his place, his goal becomes *revenge* (goal 3). Vengeful children know well where they can hurt most and proceed to do so. Being "bad" and destructive, they encourage others to treat them as they anticipate they will be treated. The ensuing abuses provide them with new justification for their antisocial stand.

Such is the case, but one must keep in mind that even these children, in their peculiar ways, are trying to integrate themselves into the group. Only their idea about how this can be done is mistaken. If our present methods of dealing with children continue, we can expect an increase in this group, which is composed of the strongest antagonists to adult society and what it stands for. Many criminals, psychopathic personalities, and social and mental deviants come from this group of children who feel that they have no place in adult society and who reject its values and regulations.

Besides these three groups of children, who more or less actively accept the challenge of adult prejudice and oppose it, there is another group whose opposition is entirely passive. Children in this group are so discouraged by the lack of faith they experience that their goal is to avoid doing anything where their anticipated inability may become apparent. They give up without even trying. Their goal is to hide behind a display of real or assumed inability in order to avoid demands (goal 4). They seem to accept their deficiency as permanent and irrevocable and thereby frustrate any educational effort to make them try, study, or apply themselves. Sometimes such passivity may be part of a power contest. Indeed, I call it "violent passivity" because it infuriates and frustrates parents and teachers. But, in any case, the more pressure adults apply, the more passive and deficient the child becomes.

Each of these four paths may be selected by a child, either as his general approach to the adult-dominated society or as a limited approach within certain group settings. Without understanding a child's goals and the purposiveness of his actions, no one can hope to deal with him effectively. Moralistic approaches are inadequate, for they do not affect either the child's goals or his role in the group.

THE PREDICAMENT OF THE TEACHER

We have seen that, generally, parents are no match for their children. They don't realize how much they are manipulated by them. And they are not familiar with the means by which children can be influenced in a democratic setting. But are the teachers in a better situation? Hardly so. They, too, are largely unaware of the extent to which their students manipulate them. Consequently, teachers still try to influence their students with traditional methods, which were effective in an autocratic society but are utterly inadequate in meeting the problems that the teachers today face. Teachers, for example, still believe that punishment can bring good results, and that those who try to act democratically are indulgent and overpermissive, that they give rise to anarchy.

There was a time, not long ago, when the teacher had the obligation to teach and the children to learn—or else. Today, this scheme does not work. Times have changed. A good example is the reluctance of our children to work with a teacher who is boring. She turns them off, and they feel justified in reciprocating by not studying.

Student self-assertion is a comparatively new phenomenon. For example, in one school all the students, asked what would have happened to their grandfathers if they had acted as the students did, admitted that their grandfathers probably would have received good thrashings. Yet children today do demand that they be entertained, and it is up to us to help teachers to become interesting and stimulating.

There are teachers, the so-called naturals, who understand children and know how to stimulate them. But they don't learn their skills in training school. We prepare teachers to teach *subjects,* not to teach *children.* Many teachers are excellent as long as the child wants to study and to behave properly. But if he decides not to do so—and an increasing number of children decide exactly that—then the average teacher does not know what to do. It is not her fault when she does not know how to reach and to correct her students, as it is not the fault of parents when they don't know how to influence a misbehaving child. Both parents and teachers are the victims of our cultural predicament, which demands that they exert their influence on the children without the tools to do it.

As a consequence, our schools are not doing their jobs. It will not do any good to spend more billions on education, or to bring education to those who are deprived of it. More of the same of what we have will never be enough. We waste our time discussing possible goals of education when we do not have the ability to get the cooperation of the students for whatever goals we set for them. We have lost control over the young.

How did it all happen? The terrific changes in our society are catching us unprepared. While this rapid change is acknowledged, its nature has not been recognized. Consequently, no adjustment has been made. Because of Dewey, probably no professional group is as aware as teachers of the need for democratic procedures. But even teachers are not familiar with the methods required in a democratic setting. They still try to influence children through punishment. They cannot imagine a classroom without grades. Our whole system of education is mistake-centered; trying to avoid or correct mistakes, instead of learning from them, is the goal.

The majority of high school students, almost everywhere in the United States, are highly critical of and antagonistic toward their teachers, even the so-called good students. Take the example of the high school student who reported that his whole class disliked a certain teacher until, one day, the teacher brought an elderly woman to the class and introduced her to the class as her mother. Suddenly the students changed their attitudes and began to like the teacher. The teacher suddenly had become a human being to them; she had a *mother*. The prejudice that students and teachers have against each other prevents them from seeing each other as human beings. "They" are enemies, and, therefore, they can be treated with all the hostility that characterizes such a relationship.

Another example involves a young boy who did not finish his work in the class and, therefore, was asked to stay after school to finish it. While he sat at his desk, the teacher worked at her table. In due time he finished, and she told him he could leave. As he left, she expressed surprise about how nice he was with her alone and how horrible he was in class. He looked up at her in astonishment: "But, teacher," he said, "I was just thinking the same about you."

Our whole educational system will need overhauling before we can be effective. John Dewey recognized this need, but, unfortunately, he went to the other extreme, and now progressive education has been discredited because of its over-permissiveness. Today we are confronted with a similar danger. Educators who reject the traditional autocratic methods, among them A. S. Neill, tend to be too permissive. With such teachers, children again run wild. Anti-authoritarian kindergartens will only lead to increased unruliness and eventually to a call for a strong man to bring order into the chaos, even if the time for tyrants has gone. A call for "law and order" and all that that expression connotes will only lead to more rebellion.

Since the present system does not work, we must search for new teaching methods. Programmed instruction through machines is highly effective, but for what reason? Is it because the child can progress on his own steam? He could do so also in a well-organized classroom, as the Montessori schools have proved. It seems that the success of the learning machine is primarily due to the fact that the child cannot fight the machine, as he does his teacher.

Eventually, the key to new methods of teaching may come from new insights into the way young children learn. It has been noted how much the child learns before he enters school and how little thereafter. For example, teachers often find it difficult to teach a child whose parents are foreign born and do not speak English. They consider dual language a handicap. Yet very young children can learn two or three languages simultaneously and in the shortest period of time. But the way young children learn is fundamentally different from the way they are taught in school. On their own they are free from the involvement of success or failure. They learn by *enjoyment*.

Difficulties in learning and behavior problems often go together. Such difficulties indicate the child's unwillingness to cooperate with the teacher. We are told that about 20–25 percent of our children never learn to read properly. Instead of recognizing in the child's inability to read the teacher's inability to teach, we constantly find new proofs of special physical conditions that excuse the teacher's failure.

There was first the question of the I.Q., which was assumed to be a reliable indicator of the child's intellectual capacity. When the reliability of the measurement was found to be faulty, then came the question of reading readiness. Since boys supposedly develop more slowly than girls, one heard the proposal that boys should learn to read at the age of eight, instead of the expected six (for girls), notwithstanding the fact that in other cultures *all* boys learn to read at the age of four. But in those places they do not yet know about the slow development of boys!

The latest discovery to excuse the teacher's failure when the child does not learn is dyslexia, the assumption of cerebral dysfunction. We also assume that there are cultural and perceptual handicaps; and hyperactivity, which prevents a child from learning, is considered the consequence of minimal brain damage.

But at the root of all our difficulties are wrong concepts about what children can do. We probably are wasting the most precious time in life by disregarding the tremendous learning capacity of very young children. It is possible that children can accumulate all the knowledge of a college graduate within the first ten years of their lives.

For example, O. K. Moore's experiments indicate that children can learn to read and write at the age of two and a half.[5] And while Moore emphasizes a difference in ability between the gifted and the average child, other experiments indicate that *all* children may be able to learn to read and write at that age. We are even told that this is the optimal age for learning to read, and that the later a child begins, the more difficult learning becomes. Glen Doman, working with brain-damaged children, found that "children can read words when they are one year old, sentences when they are two, and whole books when they are three years old,"[6] and this applies to healthy children as well, of course. According to Henry Chauncey,[7] Maria Montessori stated that the teaching of reading gets harder and harder once the child has passed the age of two; while the child past six never regains the ability he had before that age to learn to read.

Ironically, while we would assume that the discovery of the high learning potential in young children would be welcomed by the educational community, we find educators *warning* us against the great danger that may ensue from such early training.

The fear of detrimental consequences is obviously based on an unhealthy protective attitude toward children. Yet we have evidence that the greatest stimulation for the development of the child is to expose him to experiences that are

---

5. O. K. Moore, *Autotelic Responsive Environment and Exceptional Children* (Hamden, Conn.: 1963).
6. Glen Doman, *How to Teach Your Baby to Read* (New York: Random House, 1964).
7. Henry Chauncey, *Science Newsletter,* Vol. 85, 1964, p. 125.

far beyond his reach. Does such early learning deprive the child of his "childhood," as some assume? By no means. Even the most advanced prodigy who functions within his work area on an adult level is a young child in all other functions. The proposed form of learning is merely a special kind of play; it prompts intellectual activities of which children of today are deprived.

Another objection comes from those who oppose stimulation of activities, including learning, before the cerebral centers are sufficiently developed. For many years, psychoanalysts have warned about the dangers of toilet training before the central nervous system is sufficiently developed. Today we know that the cerebral maturation is not a prerequisite for functioning but its *consequence*. Only through *activities* does cerebral maturation take place.

One major breakthrough, in a completely different area, shows the extent of activity of which infants are capable. It seems that infants, until the age of six months, can swim without drowning; they have a gag-reflex that provides safeguards.[8] One can hardly visualize the far-reaching consequences this discovery will have when and if this ability to swim is recognized and utilized by parents. What does it mean? The child is *not* a helpless and almost immobile being. He is able to use all his muscles and direct his movements in water. We can well imagine how different the child's concept of himself will be in this most important formative period, and what will happen to his cerebral development if it is stimulated so early. What skills, abilities, and characteristics will be acquired, nobody can say. But as the application of these methods presupposes a different concept of children, so, in turn, these hitherto undiscovered early activities of the

---

8. M. A. Gabrielson, "Swimming Phenomenon," *Journal of Health & Physical Education Record*, Vol. 35, 1964, p. 45.

child will bring about a change in public opinion. We are, indeed, standing on the threshold of the emergence of a new type of man in a new society.

THE REVOLT OF THE ADOLESCENT

As long as children are small, warfare with adults rages only within family and school. During adolescence it is directed against society as a whole. Society faces the results of its inability to influence youth, its actions and values. Parents and teachers are blamed, but they are equally the victims when teenagers and young adults declare war on society and what it stands for.

When children reach adolescence, they must integrate themselves into society as members at large, but there is little chance for them to experience recognition and appreciation. Our competitive atmosphere induces parents to instill high ambitions in their children, but few teenagers have the opportunity to feel important through useful accomplishments. For each teenager who achieves significance through scholastic, social, or athletic success, literally thousands find no such chance. Yet they feel they have a right to be important—they want to be. Hence they try to gain status through behavior that, little appreciated by adult society, is admired by their peers. Smoking, taking drugs, driving a car wildly, making easy money, indulging in sexual activities, breaking the law— all such acts lend themselves easily to attaining a sense of importance. Yet it is at this stage that defiance of adult social values may lead to the development of psychopathic personalities.

More and more adolescents are driven to adopt hostile attitudes toward an adult society that fails to provide them with a useful place. Youngsters, looking for guidance and help, find few adults who treat them as equals and whom they can accept as friends. The more they need help and guidance, the more they are "pushed around," punished, discriminated against, and made to feel worthless. Many of them outgrow this stage and eventually find their place in adult society, particularly if they can earn money legitimately and experience respect. But many may, for the rest of their lives, remain outcasts and continue the warfare against society that began with their fight against their parents and teachers as the representatives of society.

What is called the "generation gap" is the war between the generations. It expresses itself in a difference of values. Adults object to the "lack of values" in the young; the young in turn reject adult values. Each is justified in its criticism. Many of the values prevalent in our society are more than dubious; the value system on which our young people operate is not only questionable but often outright dangerous. A whole generation of young people has developed a moral yardstick that all—the good and the bad, the successful and the failures —share: the desire for *excitement*. Boredom is intolerable, excitement the ideal. Only in the light of this value system can one fully explain the growing use of drugs.

Drugs seem to embody everything a youngster expects from life. Nothing else can provide the excitement of a "trip." Whatever the consequences, whether one is ruined for life, nothing matters. A gang of boys burglarized a house. "Why did they do it?" "We were bored." Excitement is all that counts.

The second reason for drug use has to do with a peculiar notion many young people have about finding their "identities." All they have to do, they think, in order to be definitely "different," is to do something that adults cannot stand. In their power to defeat adults they experience their "freedom," without realizing how they abuse their "rights."

For example, during a "confrontation" between a group of youngsters and some experienced Delaware counselors, the young people were asked why they liked rock and roll (which at that time was *the* rage). All agreed that they liked it because adults didn't like it. And what would they do if the adults also began to like rock and roll? "We would look for another kind of music," they said.

Today young people are again choosing the kind of music that is beyond endurance for adults. Drugs fulfill the same purpose: there is little that provokes and frightens adults more than the use of drugs by their children. And the more adults remonstrate, the more desirable drugs become.

A third factor also seems to lead to the use of drugs. Drugs induce an attitude that is similar to temporary insanity. Like a true psychotic, the user in his "mental holiday" is impervious to the demands of reality and of society. He is off in his own private world.

What are the chances for preventing the spread of the use of drugs, and of rescuing those who are involved? There is no immediate solution; the problem probably will get much worse before it gets better. Presently, no family and no community is immune from the intrusion of drugs. Powerful forces in the community keep the user enslaved. Many users want to stop taking drugs but are unwilling to change their reference group. Pressure of the peer group is too strong to resist and can be overcome only by changes in the values of the whole group. To make it worse, the problem is confounded by strong profit motives. The pushers who reap fortunes will not relinquish their hold, while their victims, trying to continue their expensive habit, see to it that nobody drops out. Society is faced with a social problem, which will have to be solved through social forces: giving youth alternatives to their "search for meaning." To this end, such self-help groups as Synanon and Daytop have a chance where outsiders fail.

One of the many contributions young people can make to society involves putting their own house in order, establishing new ideals and values, and taking on responsibility for each other. It is not enough to rebel against the faulty values of our society; youth must and will establish new and better values as its rebellion focuses attention on social ills and challenges the present educational system. Youth *is* taking on a leadership role, bringing ideals into the community, changing the sexual code, affecting the political system, but young people need to be on guard that their efforts will not be sidetracked by those who seem to rebel only for rebellion's sake.

TOWARD HARMONY BETWEEN THE GENERATIONS

Nothing can be very effective unless we terminate the war between the generations. This will take time, but it has to be done, and we have to help parents and teachers to exert their influence over their charges.

First, adults have to stop fighting, but without giving in. Neither the exertion of power nor permissiveness will bring any good results.

Second, adults must extricate themselves from the manipulation of their children. Unless they are aware of the goals of childhood misbehavior, they reinforce it, succumbing to the child's intentions instead of correcting them. They have to learn to understand the *motivation* of the child and to develop a technique for changing it.

Third, adults must employ new techniques for dealing with children, since the traditional methods are no longer effective. We have described 34 principles for raising children in a democratic society,[9] and one of the most important skills is the ability to encourage children.[10] Finally, in order to fore-

---

9. Rudolf Dreikurs & Vicki Soltz, *Children: The Challenge.*
10. Rudolf Dreikurs & Don Dinkmeyer, *Encouraging Children to Learn: The Encouragement Process* (Englewood Cliffs, N.J.: Prentice-Hall, 1963).

stall any overpermissiveness and to establish limits for the child, the technique of logical consequences has to be mastered.[11] Many adults find it difficult to distinguish between punishment and logical consequences, but a thin and very decisive line distinguishes one from the other.

Parents and teachers need to learn how to establish a democratic atmosphere, both in the home and in school. We can no longer expect to succeed by deciding for the children what they should do; we need their support. Support can only be established through group discussion. Parents need to learn how to conduct a family council, as teachers need the skill to conduct group discussions.

One advantage for the teacher is that she can make use of the classroom group. Presently teachers assume that they have the obligation to teach and correct as many as 50 *children* in a class. This is not true. The teacher is always dealing only with *one class*, regardless of whether it consists of 20 or 50 children. As group leaders, teachers can create an atmosphere that is conducive to learning. But they must learn how to integrate the class, in contrast to the present situation where the teachers intensify the gap between the good and bad students, between those who are ahead academically and those who fall behind.[12]

The group can help the teacher to solve the problems she encounters in her class. It is the group that permits her to affect the values of the students. With the support of the group, the teacher is in a position to undo all the harm the family or the community has done to the child. In the group discussion, she can make the students aware of their goals and elicit the help and understanding of all her pupils. Even in an autocratic school the teacher can establish a democratic at-

---

11. Rudolf Dreikurs & Loren Grey, *A Parent's Guide to Child Discipline* (New York: Hawthorn Books, 1970).
12. Rudolf Dreikurs, *Psychology in the Classroom* (New York: Harper & Row, 1968).

mosphere in her class by sharing the responsibility for her assignment.

Responsibility is the crucial factor in our present dilemma. The revolution that is spreading from the United States to the rest of the world, wherever the democratic process appears, is for *participation in decision-making.* Nothing short of sharing responsibility will bring about a solution to the warfare, and a first step could be to give children the right to grade their teachers. (They do it anyhow, only the teachers never know what grades they receive.)

In a camp for delinquent youth every problem was discussed with the whole group. The results were highly satisfactory. The youngsters studied and behaved. There was no need for locked doors. Then one day the principal made a decision by himself. Having found out that it was not good to have four free afternoons, he decided that there should be only two free afternoons. Immediately a riot started. The boys broke furniture, destroyed everything, refused to eat. The principal realized what he had done and arranged for an open discussion about the advantage of two instead of four free afternoons. Everyone saw his point of view and agreed with him. The students had objected only to his high-handedness.[13]

Since we are prone to give lip service to the democratic process, many American schools have a student council. However, few appreciate to what degree the student council is a travesty of democracy. The student council, generally limited in scope, carries out the orders of adults and permits representation only of the "good" students. Those who are in rebellion have little chance of being heard officially. Our schools have to become democratic before they can become effective.

---

13. Similar experiments are always successful. For example, the Gordon School in Tel Aviv, an elementary school, has full participation of the students in all school affairs. The students settle their classroom problems by themselves with the teacher as guide.

The danger of giving the students rights is that such actions can easily lead to overpermissiveness. Children may overstep their rights and neglect the necessities of the situation and their responsibilities. Therefore, the democratic process demands leadership. Parents and teachers can no longer function as bosses, but they must acquire the skill of being democratic leaders.

Finally, youth will have to be given a more active role in participation within the community. The first community function can be established by the school, in meetings between faculty, parents, and students to discuss problems that usually go beyond the difficulties of any one child. Questions of standards—how to use the car, when to come home from a date, what kind of leisure-time activity—imply differences of opinion between adults and children. These differences should be voiced during "truce" meetings, during which everyone has the right to say what he wants but also the obligation to listen to what the others have to say.

We can easily see what would happen if the principle of student participation were recognized on every level when we apply the principle to today's college scene. Our universities are—in the vast majority—undemocratic. They are run by the dictates of a president and his board of trustees. The radicals cannot accept such dictates. But they themselves are equally undemocratic, because they try to impose their will on the university. Neither the president nor the rebel has a right to decide what should be done. Whenever a university has instituted effective democratic government, student riots have become meaningless. In a democratic setting, the university's governing body should be composed of the representatives of the administration, trustees, faculties, students, and maintenance personnel. This body, alone, would have the right to make decisions. Radicals, in such a situation, would have no case. They would have the whole school population to combat. They would *already* have had a chance to be heard.

The universities, of course, need the same general overhauling of activities and principles that the lower schools need. Are they really institutions of learning? Do the students go there because they want to learn? There may be some who do, but they surely are few. Students go to college to get a degree in order to get a better job and make more money. The link between the university and economic complex is perverting the whole meaning of the university. In many cases, the graduate student is no better equipped than many who have never gone to college. With the exception of technical schools, there seems to be no correlation between a degree and competence. One graduates if one knows how to pass tests. *What* one knows is often irrelevant.

On the other hand, should the student only learn what he wants to learn? In many cases the question of relevance is one of "so-called" freedom. What we like to learn is different from what we ought to learn.

Giving in to the demands of the students is abdication; pressing them to learn what they don't want to learn is dictatorship; helping them to learn what would be beneficial for them to know requires democratic leadership.

CHAPTER 6 · **Conflict Solving in the Family**

The family is the testing ground for our attitudes and approaches in dealing with others. In the close relationships of husband and wife, of parents and children, we meet the difficulties that characterize social living in our era. All the flaws in contemporary interpersonal relationships become painfully obvious. All our mistakes and errors have immediate and unpleasant consequences for our emotional equilibrium. Consequently the family is the place where we must—and can—learn to understand the dynamics that operate between individuals; where we must—and can—develop methods that fit the new social atmosphere of a democratic society; where democratic principles must be taken from the shelf of vague general ideals and applied to the tasks of everyday living. Here is the training ground for cooperative techniques; what we learn in our families helps or hinders us in cooperating with others. The family, which reflects the old culture, becomes the cradle of the new one.

Behind the diversity and complexity of hardships, conflicts, frictions, and disturbances within the modern family lies a single pattern: the increased competition among its members. The modern family reflects the tragic confusion of a generation brought up by traditional autocratic methods that finds itself confronted with the task of establishing democratic procedures. Nobody can do this for us; each one of us has to explore, try out new ideas, use his imagination, and reconsider boldly whatever he may have thought to be definite and ultimate truth. We no longer have solid ground under our feet; we must learn to swim among uncertainties, among relative values. The easy order of right and wrong, the easy orientation to black and white, is gone forever. Yet new concepts of social and psychological interactions, vague and frightening though they may appear to those not sufficiently familiar with them, offer a wide variety of successful action once they are fully comprehended and utilized. They provide a hitherto unheard of sense of strength to those who, instead of relying on authority or definite rules, are courageous enough to trust themselves.

ARE WE VICTIMS?

Among the many pitfalls inherent in our predicament is a tendency for each of us to underestimate his strength. Oppressed by what befalls us, we cannot see what we ourselves are creating. We are impressed with the power others hold over us. They seem to force our hands and to provoke our reactions. Whatever we do wrong, we justify by what others have done to us. Good intentions we all have in abundance, but these become meaningless, for we feel frustrated at every turn. All but a few of us are convinced that we cannot be as "good" or human as we want to be because others, including our closest relatives, will not let us.

The fallacy of such impressions is obvious when we realize that each member of our family feels the same way. Each spouse blames the other for his or her troubles. Both feel frustrated by their children, who in turn feel abused by their parents and challenged by their brothers and sisters. All cannot be right in assuming that they are merely victims. Each is right from his own vantage point, but none seems to perceive how his opponent feels and what each is doing to the other in this game of mutual retaliation. A cartoon shows two dignified gentlemen meeting in a dark street, each trembling in fear that the other will accost him; neither realizes the other's panic. This is our situation. We are all afraid of each other, and we cannot understand why anyone should be afraid of us.

The first step toward improving the situation is the realization that we play an *active* part in every conflict, and that our part is the only factor we can influence. We can change no one but ourselves, but no one else's part in the conflict can remain unchanged if our part changes. The solution to a difficulty rests in our hands alone. It is useless to wait for the other fellow to take the initiative, and waiting only aggravates matters.

THE ROLE OF PRESTIGE

Behind the unwillingness to take the first step usually is our concern for prestige. Each partisan in the conflict demands that the other be the first to abandon what both must acknowledge to be improper behavior. Each would consider it a defeat and suffer a sense of humiliation should *he* be the first to move toward reconciliation of differences. It looks like appeasement, and "appeasement" is a bad word. Everyone knows that two wrongs do not make a right, but few respect this principle. On the contrary, we will not let the other fellow get away with anything! The struggle for prestige is obvious—and obviously futile. We cast aside all considerations of love, thoughtfulness, and responsibility, in our blind fear of humiliation. Oh, yes—we love one another, but we dare yield nothing. And should we do so, we then try to make a tactical withdrawal the basis of a strategic success; we bide our time until the moment of revenge.

We can extricate ourselves from this futile contest. If we begin by acknowledging the existence of the struggle for prestige, we may be able to admit that our worth depends in no way on our recognition by others, even within the family. The next step is recognition of the high price we pay for our embattled practices. Then when we consider the cost, we may abandon the contest, trusting our self-respect and respecting the opponent. So fortified, he, too, may lose the incentive for struggle. The vicious circle is broken.

THE POWER CONTEST

The process of democratization, with its ensuing competition, substituted concern with individual *prestige* for the autocratic effort to gain *power*. Our family life today reflects both the traditional tendency to overpower and the more recent cultural concern with personal prestige—an unholy alliance indeed! It makes mutual respect almost impossible. It induces all members of the family to wage war on each other. It prevents democratic organization within the family group. It stifles the most sincere desire to be fair, friendly, and compliant. It stimulates in many a desire to be the boss, and many families have far too many would-be bosses. So afraid are we of being bossed, that we decide to be bosses ourselves. Every difference of opinion becomes a contest.

Many of us still believe that no solution to a conflict other than fighting or yielding is possible. But in a democratic society, no such solutions are possible. Conflicts "solved" by subjugation breed new conflicts. The loser will not accept his defeat as permanent, and the winner is afraid of losing what he has gained. Both gird themselves for the next round. Any stable equilibrium in a democratic atmosphere presupposes mutual respect. But victors lose respect for the vanquished, and the vanquished lose respect for themselves. Nobody *has* to fight unless he wants to.

Conflicts of interest are inevitable in the close relationships of family life. They demand resolution. But most people are unaware of the many possible approaches that would avoid a power contest and permit solutions through agreement.

THE ERROR OF MORALIZING

The effects of our cultural lag are evident in the relations between parents and children. Parents find out that a child can no longer be subdued by the exercise of power. And so they rely on another form of "control," not yet aware that "control" and "influence" are very different and contradictory approaches to child rearing. Believing that the child must be "shown" what is right and wrong, parents resort to moralizing and preaching and then are surprised and helpless when these attempts at control prove to be futile. Deprived of their power to enforce obedience, unable to establish control through preaching, they are at a loss for ways to guide the child along paths they consider right and so continue with methods that are doomed in advance.

Of course, children must learn to distinguish right from wrong, to develop proper moral concepts, to embody these concepts in their consciences. But children will never learn from mere talk. Sometimes verbal communication is necessary, but the moralistic approach generally is not an effective means of communication. Can one communicate with an unreceptive child? In a moment of a transgression the child is not receptive. At the moment of conflict, words are not information but weapons. They express the wrath of a defeated authority, and angry words reveal where the parents are vulnerable. In such circumstances, for children to attempt what is forbidden is heroic. Defiance is victory, worth the sacrifice it may entail.

The issue of moral superiority is further confused by our democratic development. Children are reluctant to accept moral standards for which they see no justification. Often the standards of the parents, reflecting the time when they themselves were children, conflict with the standards prevalent among the present generation. Children feel justified in opposing parental moral judgments on the strength of their own experience and views. No longer can one simply tell a child what is right; one has to *prove* it. And this proof is often lacking, or the argument is so fallacious and intellectually untenable that the children are unimpressed.

The emergence of man as a free self-determined individual has limited the significance of conscience. We act as we are inclined to act, not necessarily as we should. With the weakening of dictatorial forces around us, motivations that are contrary to the demands of the conscience have become more important. Education must take into consideration subjective motivations that are responsible for the neglect of moral prescriptions. The child must be shown not only what is wrong but also why he continues to do what he knows is wrong. *Changing the private logic that motivates him is more effective than moral censure.* Conscience reflects outside social pressure; psychological and social stimulation are more important than moral precepts in changing behavior. We must think in terms of "motivation modification," giving children alternatives for their conduct.

THE FALLACY OF RIGHTEOUSNESS

Moral righteousness as a means of enhancing personal superiority is a steady diet in many families. Everybody wants to be "right," and everyone uses whatever intellectual capacity he has to prove himself right against his adversaries. But logic and intelligence can be used to defend any cause, good or evil. Most people can find "good" reasons for the worst causes. To resolve a conflict on the basis of who is right and who is wrong is possible only if there is an authority to decide the issue, who uses his own evaluation as a yardstick and imposes his verdict on the quarreling parties. This procedure is maintained in our courts, where the judge has the power to make the necessary decisions. Everyone knows that judicial decisions are not always "right," for they may be reversed by another judge. But if it is so difficult to establish what is right where existing laws facilitate a decision, how improbable is a "right" decision in all the complex clashes of interests between members of a family, where there is no judge entrusted with final authority—where everyone, sitting in judgment for himself, is challenged by all the others who are not on his side and who do not share his subjective point of view?

Actually, no problem or conflict that disturbs the peace of the family can be understood logically on the basis of right or wrong. The cause of the problem is psychological and social. As long as the relationship between two persons is good, no wrongdoing on the part of one of the two persons will disturb it. What counts is that neither feels personally attacked, slighted, or humiliated—or self-righteous. A mother, for instance, can excuse her child's worst offenses in school or on the playground by blaming it on the teacher or the other children. But should she get into a power contest with him, the situation changes radically and the child becomes—in her view—utterly malicious.

Unfortunately, people involved in a conflict too often are unaware of the underlying psychological problems, the disturbed relationship that alone is responsible for the friction; therefore, their efforts toward a solution are directed not toward an improvement of the relationship but rather toward fighting over the issues that arose through the disturbance in their relationship. Generally, the good arguments on which we rely for justification of our cause are only so many weapons in the battle for power. Self-righteousness is the banner of those who consider themselves the powers-that-be, who set themselves up as judges, while actually being parties to the conflict.

MUTUAL RESPECT

In a conflict, all concern with who is right and who is wrong must be discarded and replaced by methods based on a different perspective. The basis for our new vision is the recognition of the significance of relationship. Relationship is nothing fixed, nothing definite, but ever changing and fluctuating. Whatever we conceive within our society, within our family, expresses relationships and interactions. *The only stable basis for social relationships is the equilibrium between equals.* Our domestic problems present us with a task of establishing this equality; our frustrations and failures rise from our inability to do so.

A proper relationship is the basis for proper behavior. Cooperation depends on goodwill, sincere mutual interest, respect for each other. What is "right" for one relationship may be "wrong" for another, since no two situations are alike. One person may do without arousing affront what another cannot do without getting into trouble. The relativity of good and bad may be puzzling, but it is a reality with which we have to cope. *What* one does is less important than *how* one does it and under what circumstances.

Seen in this light, the essentials for living in a democratic society can be simply stated. They represent a principle that can apply to all human associations, inside and outside the home. In its simplest form, the principle implies *mutual respect, respect for the dignity of others, and respect for oneself.* The principle is expressed in a combination of firmness and kindness. Firmness implies self-respect; kindness, respect for others. Neither alone achieves a harmonious relationship of equals. If another touchstone is needed, it may be put thus:

we may resolve conflicts without either fighting or yielding—
respecting others, respecting ourselves. Being firm, unde-
feated, self-respecting, yet kind, demanding no humiliation—
these are the poles on which satisfactory human relationships
turn.

THE DYNAMICS BEHIND THE CONFLICTS

Conflicts are inevitable in any relationship because interests and goals occasionally clash. However, we must distinguish between the overt issues involved in a conflict and
the underlying dynamics of a disturbed relationship. It is not
sufficient to know the merits of the issues; nor is it sufficient
to know what we should do. We must know what we *want* to
do—and why.

Let us keep in mind the fact that the basic social motivation of each human being is the desire to belong, to have a
secure place in the group. Whatever we do reflects our concepts of social integration and participation. If we do what
the situation requires, then we obviously operate on the basis
of a correct evaluation of the situation. On the other hand,
each wrong step and disturbing act reflects mistaken concepts about participation and erroneous interpretations of
the current conflicts. Knowing this, we can train ourselves to
look at a conflict as it appears to our opponents. We can
learn to become sensitive to their private logic, if we wish to
understand it. Our success in solving conflicts depends largely
on our ability to see things from the other's point of view.
Success, then, requires empathy, a natural response that is
usually stifled by antagonism. But we may not be willing
really to understand an opposing point of view because understanding and empathy may prevent us from fighting as
vigorously as we deem necessary to preserve our "rights."
Understanding can preclude hostility.

In order to understand each other, we need to think in

terms of the *purpose* of human actions. Unfortunately, we cannot ascertain a person's goals by asking him because he does not know what his purpose is. Children very persistently pursue their goals, without the slightest awareness of what they are doing. They need help to understand their goals.

Familiarity with the four goals of misbehaving children can enable the adult to recognize them and to understand the private logic of the child, according to which he acts. Unfortunately, the goals of adults are not so simple and obvious. Nevertheless, we can be sure that beneath the antagonism and opposition of adults are some of the same elements that motivate the child to increase his demands and to defy those around him. If we are interested in promoting solutions to our conflicts, we can become sensitive to the needs of others to feel important, respected, and appreciated. We can see beneath their overt action of aggression or neglect their feeling of defeat and their attempt to retaliate, their fear and discouragement. Nobody misbehaves as long as he believes in his ability to succeed by useful means. Discouragement and fear are the prime factors behind any socially unacceptable behavior. The overt demonstration of superiority barely conceals intensive self-doubt, the sense of inadequacy that one tries to hide from others, the indefatigable effort to be "more" or be "better." Once we are trained to see and to comprehend this insecurity in the other members of our families, we can avoid retaliation, which only increases the original fears, inferiority feelings, and mistaken forms of compensation. We can actually learn to alleviate their problems—not by words but by actions.[14] Thus telling someone that he is

---

14. This is a most important precaution in the use of psychology. Anything that is very effective can also become dangerous, if not properly used. However little training one may have in psychology, it cannot do any harm as long as this knowledge is not expressed in words but is taken as a basis for action. It is possible to use psychological explanations in the family, but only in a meeting of the family council—and then, too, with caution.

suffering from an inferiority complex, or that he is trying to be the boss or to be superior, is empty name-calling. But we can help a person to overcome such problems, mistaken goals, and attitudes through *encouragement* and other psychologically effective actions.

IMPROVING THE RELATIONSHIP

Behind any open conflict lies a disturbed relationship, and trying to solve the conflict is an impossibility unless sincere efforts are first made to establish a friendly atmosphere. We are always more willing to do things for people we like than to respond to justified requests when we feel antagonistic. The merits of a request are of little importance in comparison with how we feel about the person making the request. A new perspective evolves from these considerations. Right and wrong take on a different meaning. The *field of action* becomes more significant than the issue itself. The total situation emerges as the real issue; *an individual act can be understood only within the total setting.*

It is essential to arrange pleasant experiences for both parties together, husband and wife, parents and children. Common pleasant activities help to prepare the atmosphere so that agreements can be reached without winners or losers, without anyone's feeling imposed upon or humiliated. Conflicting ideas and interests should be discussed only when everyone feels friendly. If conflict is involved, the discussion should take place only in the family council, and the first thing the members of the family have to learn to do is to listen. Everyone has the *right* to say what he thinks and also the *obligation* to listen to what the others say, trying to understand what the other fellow feels and thinks. In this way, every problem and conflict becomes a common problem. Otherwise, no solution is possible.

There is another important principle in finding solutions.

To think only in terms of what the *other* person should do leads to a dead end. We can maintain an open road only if we think in terms of what *we* can do in a given situation.

Even if there is no chance of finding a perfect solution, there is always a way to improvement, regardless of the intensity of the conflict. No situation is so hopeless that it does not permit alternatives. If we are willing to do what can be done under existing circumstances, we may find ourselves on the way to a real solution.

In many cases, indeed, we may not know what to do at all. A simple expedient may then help. We usually know what we should *not* do. If we refrain from doing it, we are generally launched on the right course. What, then, ought we not do? Whatever will worsen our relationship, humiliate and frustrate our opponent. We may have our hands full keeping ourselves from doing just this. Yet, this self-restraint is often sufficient to bring about eventual agreement. Furthermore, our concern with *our own course* of action removes the pressure from the other person and gives him an opportunity to think what *he* could do to improve the situation.

Though we may be willing to see the benefits of these approaches when we are dealing with adults, most parents still consider them inapplicable to children. There, they feel, immediate action is needed. Yet, when they take immediate action, they generally do not get far; for the same principles apply to interactions between adults and children. Only when life is in danger is immediate action imperative, and such occasions occur far less frequently than overanxious parents assume. Immediate action is sometimes possible and even necessary in dealing with children, but no constructive end is served by the retaliatory actions—usually unpleasant words —to which most parents feel provoked.

Our general relationship to children needs careful reconsideration—and improvement. Love is not sufficient. *Love does not guarantee respect.* This important fact is often overlooked by those who think that love alone will give children "security." Security means belief in one's strength, and love does not provide the child with such an experience. We must learn to treat children with *respect*. This prime prerequisite for a proper relationship implies expression of our respect—in words and deeds, in the tone of voice, in the willingness to *listen* for their feelings and intentions, even when we do not agree with them. *Respect does not imply subservience.* Showing respect implies being a good friend, not *demanding* trust, not bribing, but *earning* friendship. And one does not win the friendship and regard of a child by humiliating him or giving in to his whims.

ENCOURAGEMENT

Our efforts to resolve conflicts must go beyond the establishment of good, friendly relations. Most disturbing behavior on the part of adults and children alike is the result of discouragement. Only a courageous person can face issues squarely and deal with them effectively. We constantly encourage or discourage those around us and thereby contribute materially to their greater or lesser ability to function.

In keeping with our penchant for self-concern, we may find it easier to recognize the far-reaching effect of encouragement when we are the recipients. We all know how differently we behave in different company. With some we are at our best; with others we feel inhibited, cannot find the right words, act clumsily, and feel inadequate. What makes the difference is the encouragement or discouragement we receive. Interestingly enough, we may be discouraged not only by a person who—we think—dislikes and belittles us but also by one who seems to expect too much from us. In any case, if we are not sure of ourselves, we fail to utilize all our inner resources. In short, one person puts us at ease while another makes us tense, because one increases our faith in ourselves while the other undermines it.

It is not difficult to see that happen *to* us, but we seldom realize that we exercise a similar influence *on* others. We make every person with whom we come in contact feel better or worse, by encouraging or discouraging him. We bring out the best or worst in those we meet, merely by our attitudes and our expectations. We must realize that as we respond to others, we influence them, too.

This principle is of utmost importance in dealing with children. Children need encouragement as a plant needs sun and water. The process of growing up, especially in our era with its characteristic tendency to indulge and to humiliate, implies a series of discouraging experiences. Unless we deliberately offset this cultural tendency, we fail as parents and as educators. When the child is already so discouraged that he behaves badly, encouragement is particularly imperative. Unfortunately, the worse the child behaves and the more encouragement he needs, the less he is likely to receive. It is not easy to encourage a disturbing child because he discourages us. Yet until we change *our* attitudes, we cannot help our children.

The ability to encourage seems to be the most important single quality in getting along with others. This is why, to the amazement and despair of responsible adults, so many "wrong" people gain so much influence on children and adolescents. It seems as if those who induce children to perform anti-social actions know more about encouragement than those whose responsibility it is to promote healthy growth and development.

The ability to encourage presupposes faith in oneself. If that faith is lacking, our compensatory desire for self-evaluation will defeat our best efforts. People who are too kind, pay false compliments, and make an undue fuss do not encourage; they merely condescend. Children see through their facade and realize the insincerity behind it.

The ability to encourage is the ability to instill self-confidence. Nobody has enough self-confidence. Everyone's picture of himself is to some degree fallacious, and no one is free from the conviction that he is not good enough. In order to change any person's mistaken self-concept, *we* must be sincerely convinced that *he* is *good enough as he is*. We all *could* be better than we are, but this does not mean that *unless* we become better we will never be worthy.

The dynamic factor in growth is courage. No one can become skilled or competent unless he first believes in his ability to become so. Yet we assume that we have to point out faults and deficiencies in ourselves and others in order to help and correct. We are impressed by the need to avoid mistakes in order to avoid humiliation. We are all conditioned to be afraid of mistakes. Regardless of what we do well, a mistake may undo everything. In an autocratic society conformity is taken for granted, deviation not tolerated, and such concepts have been carried over into the competitive atmosphere of today. Every mistake is held to endanger status.

The negative evaluation of mistakes leaves little room for encouragement. Half-hearted efforts to tell a child how much better he could do will only confirm the underlying criticism that he does not measure up. We must realize that we *cannot build on deficiencies, only on strength*. We cannot help our children—or anyone else—to have faith in themselves as long as *we* have no faith in them.

THE NEED FOR SELF-RESPECT

The need to increase others' self-esteem should never lead to the belief that their self-esteem means everything, our own nothing. Such "unselfishness" is not "goodness" but false pride. We are an integral part of every situation, of every conflict. Denying ourselves the pursuit of our interests does not make us cooperative, but merely submissive. One cannot establish a good relationship on the basis of submission and appeasement. One does not gain respect in this way, and without mutual respect no harmonious and lasting equilibrium is possible.

Integrating our interests with those of others is one of the most difficult tasks of our time. We have no precedent. Opposition of ideas and interests does not have to lead to conflict or "compromise." Compromise is not necessarily agreement; both parties can feel defeated or cheated, with subsequent bitterness. Equilibrium between equals requires *mutual consent* and *agreement*. Only a subtle line separates self-assertion from imposition, considerateness from submission. And yet the consequences of one or the other are as widely different as friction and harmony, friendliness and hate, war and peace.

On what does the harmonious equilibrium of equals hinge? On a principle close to that expressed in the old adage: "Mind your own business." This maxim does not necessarily mean that we should not be concerned with others and the common welfare. It expresses both an obligation and a privilege. We must have the courage and stamina to do what *we* think is right, taking into consideration the interests and needs of others, but we have *no right* to tell others what *they* ought to do. Independence and interdependence are not mutually exclusive, but rather complementary. To have strong and definite ideas, interests, and convictions does not preclude cooperation; it enriches every relationship. We can be respected for our stand if we proceed properly.

APPLYING NATURAL CONSEQUENCES

This principle of minding our own business provides useful guidance to parents who are searching for ways to stimulate their children to respect order and the needs of others.

Just as in adult relationships, it is difficult to distinguish between the requirements of a situation and our personal preferences. Thus, parents find it difficult to distinguish between the rights of their children to self-determination and their own right to order. But by minding their business and permitting the "natural consequences" of a situation to impose their own pressures, parents can help their children to grow up with respect for others without a feeling of submission or humiliation. This approach, *substituting the demands inherent in a given situation for parental authority,* induces children to respect order out of consideration for their own interests and not in submission to their parents' demands. Instead of emphasizing pressure from without, it evokes a proper motivation from within. It eliminates the need for reward and punishment. It permits agreement for the benefit of all, without fight and submission. It sets the *necessary limits* for the child.

To adults, the difference between punishment and natural consequences is often difficult to perceive; for them, unpleasant results remain unpleasant regardless of whether they are imposed by circumstances or by a person. Not so for children. If the logic of reality is permitted to operate, the child is left with the freedom to choose, and he feels respected if his parents let him choose. Then he is more willing to do what is good for all. Preaching and scolding are eliminated, as the parents stand by patiently and let the child grow into accepting his responsibility.

To take an example, there is no one living who does not want to eat—except our children. At mealtimes parents often demand that their child eat all the food on his plate and in turn become worried and angry if he refuses to eat at all. But nobody has the right to force another person to eat; the excuse that not eating a meal or a given food will endanger the child's health is flimsy. The mother's pressure, instead of stimulating his appetite, *prevents* the child from eating. In any case, the child has the right to refuse food. But, alternatively, he does not have the right to demand that special food be served to him. When mothers yield, as they do too often, by giving the child either special attention or service in order to "make him eat," they are making themselves slaves to the child at the same time that they are trying to overpower him.

Similarly, a child has the right to come to the table with dirty hands, but the mother has no obligation to serve him if his hands are dirty. The child has a right to leave his toys or other belongings lying around, but he has no "right" to demand that his mother take care of them for him or keep after him to "remind" him to move them. The mother may put the child's things away—somewhere—if she finds them in her way, and if the child misses them afterward and is upset, he has brought the consequences on himself. All this can be done in a friendly spirit, without hard words and hostility. Indeed, the absence of hostile emotion distinguishes natural consequences from punishment.[15] The child knows in advance what to expect and can orient himself accordingly.

The principle of natural consequences can best be applied at home, but it is also possible to apply it in the classroom, under certain conditions. As long as we submit to anyone, we cannot expect to be respected by him. As long as we let others abuse us, they will take advantage of our weakness and force us into submission. If we are intimidated, we will find it impossible to assert ourselves in a friendly but firm manner. No retaliation on our part will make up for our submission. At the same time, we have no right to demand submission from others in any relationship. If we disapprove of a person's action, we can remove ourselves, or reconsider our own course of action, without arguments or fights. The pressure

---

15. This distinction is most difficult for parents who feel defeated and try to impose their will on the child. The best "natural" consequence is turned into ineffective punishment if the attitude of the parents is retaliatory and punitive.

of reality will induce all participants to consider their common interest if submission by either party is ruled out.

Gandhi's principle of nonviolent resistance reflects basically this formula. We are not here to tell anyone what *he* should do, or to let anyone tell us what *we* should do. In making our definite stand known, we can be forceful without dominating; we can maintain our interests without imposing on others. We can resist force and aggression without fighting; we cannot combat violence with violence. The right to self-direction is a basic right and we must guard it carefully, and, logically, we can claim this right for ourselves only if we grant it to everyone else.

ORDER AND FREEDOM

By the exercise of choice a child develops a feeling of self-determination that any self-respecting individual in a democratic atmosphere not only needs but demands, but it is difficult for parents to realize what a wide range of decisions a child is capable of making for himself. Instead, parents restrict a child and let themselves be restricted by him. Almost all questions of routine in daily living can become the focus of controversy. These include the most elementary decisions: the time to go to bed, what to wear, what to do in free time, what to play, when and what to eat, how to talk and how to walk, what to say and what not to say. We all impose—or try to impose—our will on others. And none of us is free to do as he sees fit, since whatever he does is opposed by someone else. There is no freedom—and no order. We must get used to the idea that in a democratic atmosphere freedom and order are inseparable.

We are slow in recognizing this fact because it has only recently been experienced in our culture. In the autocratic past "freedom" meant disregard for order; it was the slogan under which people fought against tyranny—and finally won.

Today we have gained much freedom, but we still tend to use it in opposition to order. And we are raising a generation of children who believe that "freedom" means doing as they please. When parents give the impression—perhaps not in words but in actions—that cooperation means "Do what I want you to do," it is not surprising that the child soon learns to imitate them, and demands in turn, by his behavior, that his parents do as *he* pleases.

Words alone cannot persuade children that order is beneficial to all, even to them. A practical application of the natural consequences when order is disturbed is more convincing. When Johnny rebels against some of his responsibilities, for example, his mother can take him aside and ask him how he would feel if for the next week he could do whatever he wanted. Every boy would rejoice at such a prospect; it is too good to be true. Then his mother asks, "If you can do as you please, do you mind if I also do as I please?" Again, Johnny probably consents without hesitation since, to most children, parents do as they please, anyhow. And so the next day arrives. Johnny has anticipated it with joy. But when he comes for his breakfast, his mother does not feel like getting up. He has to find whatever he can for himself. He takes this small problem in his stride because he feels free, and that is worth the price. But when he comes home for lunch and his mother has had lunch out with a friend and the refrigerator is empty and Johnny is hungry, the situation is not so bright. And when, during the day, sundry occasions arise when Johnny wants something from his mother and she does not feel inclined to acquiesce, he begins to think twice. Before the day is over, Johnny may have a new idea of what order means. He may suddenly realize that order is not only for the benefit of the parents, as most children assume.

Too rarely do our children have a chance to experience the logic of order. And seldom do we realize that we cannot enjoy freedom unless we grant it to others. Only if every member of the family is sure of his freedom as an equal member of the group can each be expected to give his best for the common good, to respect the order that is necessary for all. Otherwise resentment, rebellion, and usurping of rights at the expense of others make harmony and order impossible.

Equality, which we all desire and for which we strive, poses to all of us great and new problems. Democracy must start at home. If we cannot have equality within the family, where else can we expect it? The new order requires that each person share with every other the responsibilities for the whole. Husband and wife and each of the children may take on different functions, according to individual abilities and inclinations. But each desires full appreciation, regardless of what he is or does.

In such circumstances, ideal but not unobtainable, order is no longer the concern of one or two, but of all, each one participating in its establishment, experimenting and exploring all avenues until those best suited for the common good are found. Then we have a natural order based on freedom for all and on a sense of responsibility that characterizes free men everywhere. Then we know the freedom so well described by Robert Francis in his poem, "Seagulls."

> What we have labored all our lives
> To have, and failed,
> These birds effortlessly achieve:
> *Freedom that flows in form and still is free.*

Perhaps in no other area of social living is the rapid progress toward equality as obvious as in the relationship between the sexes. The difficulties we encounter are not the
consequence of the *inequality* women labor under but of the
equality that women have achieved. It is true that equal
rights do not yet exist and will have to be established. But
women do not realize that the rights of women have been
recognized much earlier and more fully than the rights of
Negroes and of children. (As far as children are concerned,
their "needs" have been recognized but never before their
claim for treatment as equals.)

During most of our civilization's history society has been
patriarchal. According to ancient Jewish law, for example, a
husband can divorce his wife for adultery, but infidelity on
his part gave his wife no right to divorce him. In many feudal
societies the wife could be divorced if she bore no son. But
the male has not always been dominant. There is historical
evidence that, in the early phases of our civilization, certain
matriarchal cultures in Greece, Crete, and Egypt awarded
women many privileges denied to men. Even some primitive
societies, which cannot be easily compared with civilized cultures, gave—and give—women dominant rights.

The dominance may have changed from one sex to the
other, but at no time—except for a few instances of limited
scope—has there been equality between the sexes approxi-
mating that which exists today, particularly on the American
scene. The present degree of equality between the sexes cor-

responds to the growing tendency toward equality in all other areas of personal and group relationships. And as in the other areas, the process is still going on, and the ensuing friction is the source of many of our most urgent domestic problems.

THE FOUR RIGHTS OF THE DOMINANT SEX

Four rights have been the exclusive privilege of one sex, whenever its dominance was firmly entrenched: political, economic, social, and sexual. Until recently, only men enjoyed these rights and privileges. They alone had political power, with the few exceptions of feminine rulers in otherwise male-dominated governments. Men alone could possess, will, or inherit property. The social position of woman depended entirely on that of the man on whom she depended—father, husband, or brother. Woman had no sexual "rights"; man all. Rigid religious and secular laws *demanded* purity and monogamy; yet the restrictions were *applied* only to women. Social conventions permitted men pre- and extramarital relationships. If a woman lost her "virtue," she lost everything—respect, social status, even her place in family and society. For men, it was almost obligatory to have sexual "experience" before entering marriage.

Now let us examine our present situation. *Political* equality of suffrage has been achieved, and women can be elected to office, though few of us can imagine a Congress consisting of a majority of women and most of us accept the present masculine majority without much objection. Only in the last few years has there been serious discussion of the possibility of a woman becoming president of the United States. Political equality between the sexes is growing, but it has not yet been fully achieved.

Regarding *economic* equality between the sexes, much has been made of the fact that most of the wealth in the United

States is owned by women. Women may now inherit property and will it. The husband no longer owns whatever his wife earns or receives. But women do not yet have *complete* economic equality. Most of the wealth possessed by women is managed by men. High economic positions are almost exclusively held by men. Despite exceptions, the wages for women are still generally lower than those for men in the same positions. In a time of unemployment, it is still the woman who is expected to give up her job, under such rationalizations as are always found to support social conventions in favor of the dominant group.

It is perhaps more difficult to recognize that women have *not* yet gained the same *social* rights as men. True, their social position no longer depends on that of their husband, father, or brother. They can climb or descend the social ladder on their own merit. A woman who marries a man below her in status does not necessarily sink to his social level; she may elevate him to her position. Women do, however, assume the husband's name, a traditional sign of patriarchal structure socially, and divorce affects a woman more adversely than a man, though in this area, too, conditions are rapidly changing.

Discussion of *sexual* rights is a precarious undertaking. Established sexual morals are regarded by many as so fundamental that any deviation, as a result of social change or whatever, is considered amoral and offensive. Moral concepts, however, do reflect social conventions and change with each culture. Legal and moral conventions are not imposed upon man by any authority outside himself; they are man-made. Nevertheless, the contemporary social changes toward democracy are inevitably producing new moral standards, and no authority can stay this process.

The growing equality between the sexes is responsible for the gradual breakdown of the double standard for sex activities, heretofore largely accepted by men and women alike. On the one hand, the demand that men now be as chaste as women, attributed to Puritan influence, is an expression of growing equality between the sexes. Stricter observance of monogamy is one way of depriving man of his one-sided privilege. On the other hand, as restrictions are imposed on men, bringing them to the level of chastity previously demanded from women, so the democratic evolution has led to new freedoms for women. Participating in increasing numbers in industry and commerce and—for the first time in history—serving in the armed forces with equal rank to men, women have taken upon themselves the right to be sexually as free as men. Society is changing its conventions and beginning to accept women in a new role. As a sign of this change, the stigma attached to an unwed mother is fast diminishing, so that a woman who decides to bring up a child who has no legal father no longer loses her self-respect or her social status.

The sexual code for women varies greatly with each community and is influenced by racial and national compositions, economic and educational levels, and prevalent religious orientations. These factors largely determine the rights of women, and wherever woman is accepted as an equal, she acts with greater sexual latitude. This freedom implies not merely greater laxity but also greater aggressiveness. Under patriarchal conditions women were supposed to be passive, to wait, to be chosen, although they learned to direct men's decisions in many subtle but effective ways. Today, however, many men are worried that women may become the dominant sex as they gain independence and privileges. Indeed, women have already become, in many regards, the dominant sex, at least in the family.

The change in the status of women has actually affected their approach to marriage. As long as women could find their place only through marriage, they tried their best to get married. Today, women hesitate before marriage as often as, and as much as, men—and sometimes more. In the choice of a mate they are more confused than their sisters of yesterday.

Then the choice was simple, especially since it often was out of the girl's hands altogether. Her parents acted on her behalf; any male who could support a wife and did not show any glaring faults and defects was considered a good prospect. Today the girl herself chooses; the standards are more complex. Two factors confuse modern girls: one often a conscious consideration—so-called romantic love—the other an inner conflict of which most are not aware—male-female competition.

ROMANTIC LOVE

Confusing and yet characteristic of the growing equality of women is the importance attached to romantic love. Sociologists and psychiatrists have long recognized that love alone is not an adequate basis for the choice of a mate. When there were fewer opportunities for the girl and she had virtually no choice, other qualifications of pairing were considered more important. Falling in love, often merely an expression of physical attraction, was not then—nor is it now—enough to assure fulfillment in marriage. When the first intoxication is over and husband and wife find themselves confronted with each other as persons and not as enthusiastic lovers, they often find that they have little in common. The ensuing disappointment frequently hampers their willingness to adjust to each other. Mutual interests, common backgrounds, corresponding personality traits, on the other hand, may eventually evoke a deep and lasting love, based on a strong feeling of belonging and of wanting each other. Ironically, when women marry only the men with whom they have "fallen in love," they imitate the masculine manner of choosing a partner: in a patriarchal setting physical attractiveness is the main asset of a woman. Under such conditions no man has to worry about his bride's personality traits; he has every reason to expect her to do as he wants anyhow. And since the bride is supposed to be innocent and inexperienced, it is up to him to shape her personality to his own liking.

The search for romantic love expresses modern woman's quest for sexual and sensuous gratification. We have evidence that frigidity is relatively common when sex gratification is considered a "natural" prerogative of men, and women merely a means to provide it. To a degree in various cultures it was considered improper for women to become sexually aroused— even by their husbands. "Good wives" were without any sexual desires or demands, and the sex hunger of modern women, freeing themselves of the traditional shackles of past centuries, presents our generation with new problems, both before marriage and after. And while oversexed men could always find willing submissive subjects, the demands of women on masculine performance may create more serious problems.

COMPETITION BETWEEN THE SEXES

The second factor affecting and confusing the minds of many modern girls when they think of marriage is even more destructive. To make it worse, they often are not even aware of the problem and are therefore perplexed by their subsequent marital tribulations.

Modern woman faces a peculiar predicament. On one hand, she is the product of thousands of years of feminine submission. Consequently, she still looks for the superior man on whom she can lean, who is strong, reliable, and capable of protecting her. In her growing years she may have experienced such a man in the person of her father, the last remnant of masculine superiority. And she may seek such a superior male as a mate. But he is hard to find. It is difficult for any man to be superior to a girl who has had the same education, worldly experience, and training as he, and who, in many instances, may have been more successful than her male peers. On the other hand, modern woman is also the product of the twentieth century, a human being who does not want to be inferior and submissive to anyone.

The consequences of the predicament often are disastrous. She may avoid any strong male who threatens to dominate her and marry someone who succumbs to her superiority, then complain bitterly that her husband is not a "real" man whom she can respect. Or she may yield to one who seems to be strong and superior, then endeavor in her marriage to prove to herself and to him that his "superiority" is a sham. In the ensuing disillusionment he appears to be a weakling, or, if he successfully resists her efforts to "cut him down to size," a bully. In any case, the struggle for superiority and domination replaces cooperation and mutual respect, often with fatal consequences for the marriage.

Whether or not both partners appreciate the extent of their mutual efforts to gain superiority, marriage today is often the battleground on which husband and wife, each dubious about his own place, fight for dominance. All predicaments and hardships serve as tests. Yet, financial difficulties, in-laws, sexual problems, infidelity, incompatibility— whatever may be considered as the cause for marital trouble— is not in fact the *cause* of trouble but the *occasion* at which each feels defeated. As long as the relationship between husband and wife is friendly, as long as they are not in competition and do not resent each other, difficulties and predicaments bring them closer together and stimulate their common effort to deal with the dilemma. But in an atmosphere of rivalry and competition, each blames the other for their common plight; each feels neglected, humiliated, or abused, and consequently each makes the partner feel unfairly criticized and rejected.

In the past it was the men who frequently sought separation and divorce; in recent years it is more often the women. This fact, of course, reflects woman's greater independence, her realization that even without a man she can now maintain her place in society, but there is a more serious implication. The increase in the divorce rate attributable to women's dissatisfaction is evidence of the fact that men often fail to come up to the standards women are now setting. There was a time when women wanted to be as good as any man; today they want to be better. Women are becoming so "good" that their husbands and children have great difficulty in amounting to something, at least within the family.

MAN'S RESPONSE

It is difficult for a man to extricate himself from the traditional assumption that he is superior to woman *by nature*. Is he not taller, physically stronger, endowed wth a deeper voice and a larger brain? Although women's athletic records may soar above those previously established by men, the top achievement in sports in most fields is still held by men. Therefore, are not men entitled to a superior social role and to a "natural" position of dominance in the relationship between the sexes?

The assumption of a "natural" masculine superiority has always been a threat to women *and* to men. Adler coined the term "masculine protest" to indicate how women rebel against an assumed masculine superiority, and men feel frustrated by their assumed superiority, uncertain of their own masculine prowess and unable really to feel like the strong men they were supposed to be. Actually, man's superior physical strength and height may be merely the result of traditional patterns of mating. It may well be that women felt embarrassed at being coupled with shorter men and that men chose smaller spouses. In the process of "natural selection" tall women had difficulty in finding mates. Whatever the reason, since the trend toward equality permits women to marry shorter men, and men have begun to choose older and even bigger partners, the sex determination of height and strength may well slowly disappear.

The change in masculine and feminine patterns causes considerable confusion, both to boys and to girls. A new concept of feminine superiority, based on intellectual and moral qualities, is emerging, and it leads to a new "feminine protest." Concurrently, however, women increasingly feel that they cannot live up to *the* feminine ideal, often presented to them by their mothers, and men resent the newly emerging superiority of women.

Actually, by renouncing the obligation to play a superior role, men free themselves from an almost intolerable burden, if only they knew it. As long as man clings to the myth of masculine superiority, he can never live in peace with women who constantly, and with increasing success, challenge every vestige of that "superiority."

MUTUAL SUSPICION

In the circumstances, it is difficult for the sexes to recognize their essential equality. Men often cannot believe that they themselves are esteemed and appreciated; women are prone to assume that they themselves are dominated and subdued. Every disagreement in the social and sexual function, every argument, from highly intellectual contentions to trivial daily occurrences, offers ample opportunity to inject the question of who is the boss. As long as a man or a woman is not sure of his own value and equal status, each assumes defeat by a partner who feels equally defeated. It is hard for each to believe that the other shares the same sense of failure. Each is afraid of the other and cannot see why the other should have any reason to be afraid of him. And the eternal struggle between the sexes is injected into every predicament, controversy, and difference of opinion; it not only precludes the possibility of a solution but engenders hostility and distrust be-

tween two groups that cannot live without each other and
have not learned to live peacefully with each other.

An incident may demonstrate this intrinsic tendency to
inject the "battle between the sexes" into every form of interaction. Many years ago in Vienna I had lectured to a women's
group about equality and the rights of women. The chairman
of the meeting expressed her delight in having found a man
who did not assume masculine superiority. According to her,
very few men respected women. I disputed this claim and assured her that I knew many men who shared my opinion.
Maybe it was she who looked for humiliation—and perhaps
provoked it—I suggested.

There was no opportunity at the time to pursue this discussion. But she was an educator, and we were both interested
in the same problems, so she invited me to tea to exchange
our experiences. As we discussed various aspects of child guidance and personality development, it became obvious that we
operated on different and contradictory scientific premises.
She was a Freudian; I an Adlerian. The discussion became
hotter. Each defended his own position and challenged that
of the other. Suddenly, my hostess interrupted the discussion
to voice her disappointment in me. She had thought that I—
in contrast to other men—had respect for a woman and her
opinion, but now she could see that I, like the rest, was only
interested in establishing my own masculine superiority over
her.

Yet all we had done was to discuss conflicting psychological
theories in the same way that two men would have done.

INCOMPATIBILITY

Whether incompatibility in interests or incompatibility in
sex is blamed for marital failure, the frequency of such com-
plaints clearly demonstrates the effects of equality in modern
family life.

Differences of interests do not necessarily disturb a relationship. A young girl in love is more than willing to follow her young man's interests, even if they are foreign to her. She accompanies him to ball games without any previous knowledge of the sport, and before long she may enjoy it as much as he. Her ability to participate in his interests depends on their relationship. Indeed, both partners in a marriage can stimulate new interests in each other. But once they reach a stage in which both feel neglected, their different inclinations and tastes are used by one to feel rejected and by the other to feel imposed upon.

Thus the frequent discrepancy in interests between men and women is often the result of their competition. Men still attempt to reserve certain activities, such as politics, business, and sports, to themselves. For here they feel safe in a "man's world." Likewise, women, more than men, are interested in fine arts, theater, literature, psychology, and education. Such interests are possibly the result of women having a greater amount of leisure time than men, but, in any case, the interests do provide women with a sense of superiority.

Differences of interests *can* enrich a marriage, when the vision of each partner broadens the vision of the other, but a division of interests that serves as a competitive weapon is highly destructive. The wife may "try" to induce her husband to participate in intellectual, cultural, and social activities but may unwittingly use her background and training as a subtle assertion of her superiority. Instead of encouraging her husband, she may make it almost impossible for him to follow her lead. Impressed with his inability to keep up with her and concerned with the preservation of his masculine superiority, he may avoid situations where he can only play second fiddle. Thus many successful businessmen and executives shy away from social activities because they can function only when they are on "top," and they have not developed the skill to shine at parties or social gatherings.

Literature and art offer many opportunities for mutual enjoyment. But the wife's perfectionism, her impatient and eager criticism, may prevent her husband's enjoying them. Similarly, many men deplore their wives' lack of business sense, yet become resentful when their wives have and use it. In a competitive relationship each partner finds it difficult to acknowledge the other's ability.

SEXUAL DISSATISFACTION

It seems that full sexual gratification is found less frequently in than outside marriage. But here again, dissatisfaction is less the cause of marital discord than the result of it. It does not necessarily reflect a clash of personalities, temperaments, and inclinations; for the same two people can have highly satisfying sexual experiences at the beginning of their marriage and later become unable to satisfy each other—all without any real change in their personalities.

The term "incompatibility" assumes that there are basic discrepancies, but such discrepancies often do not exist at all. Naturally, sexual temperament and training vary in any two adults. Two people who meet in marriage cannot possibly have the same past experiences and attitudes. But these differences can be utilized to the advantage of both, each supplementing and enriching the other. As long as both partners want to please each other, each can adjust to the other's desires, training, and needs. In this mutual adaptation both partners change and find a common ground for enjoyment. Consequently, it is no accident that many sexual difficulties arise later in marriage, when antagonisms and frictions have piled up; for then the most intimate union that requires full cooperation has ceased.

The newly acquired equality of women also is a disquieting factor. In the past, sexual frustrations were probably less frequent. Men had no difficulties in finding gratification, and they cared little for what women desired. Sex was their right by social consent, and women were merely useful. Women recognized and accepted their obligation to serve men as sexual objects. It was their "duty" to submit, regardless of how they felt. Today, having gained the status of full-fledged members of society, women demand the same right of gratification.

It is impossible for two people to always want the same thing at the same time and to the same extent. As long as the relationship is good and harmonious, differing demands pose no problem. But in the strife for mutual equality differences are the occasion for contest. Marriage is considered a "50-50" proposition, and this assumption is at the root of most marital problems. Each partner is constantly watching to ensure that he gets his 50 percent and is afraid of getting only 49—or less. Yet a harmonious marriage is possible only if each mate is willing to give 100 percent—all he has. Only then is he able to look at any contingency as a challenge he can meet.

The limited commitment to marriage has a direct bearing on the sexual function. As soon as one partner wants more than the other, both feel abused. One feels rejected and the other imposed upon, and once this stage is reached, a vicious circle starts. To prove his rights and point to the other's lack of cooperation, one partner increases his demands, and the other, in resentment, becomes more reluctant to give in.

Concern with "success" and "failure" disturbs the sexual function even further. It is impossible to function fully in a sexual relationship if one partner is preoccupied with extraneous problems, and concern with one's "adequacy" necessarily inhibits one's sexual performance. Thus the fact that in times of increased women's equality men become impotent or seek escape into homosexuality is not mere coincidence. Homosexuality is a cultural phenomenon, as was the case in classical Greece when the democratic process affected woman's status.

Obviously concern over success leads to the desire for perfection. Whatever we do has to be "just right"; otherwise, we are failures. This attitude, too, injects a disturbing note into marital sex activities. Each act should be "perfect." Deviation from that standard becomes distressing, particularly to women. Even if they do something wrong, it has to be done "in the right way." In this area of intimate interaction, all the flaws in interpersonal relations become accentuated. At work and in social contacts it is possible to get by with limited co-operation; there is no need to *give* oneself. Marriage does not permit such distance; it requires that we give ourselves completely, an impossibility if we are tense, fearful, and apprehensive. Sex fulfillment presupposes the ability to relax and to enjoy.

INFIDELITY

The disturbed sexual relationship in marriage and the desire for escapades and sexual "victories" make infidelity more common. In modern marriage, as contrasted with those in the past, infidelity poses an increasingly serious problem. In the past, masculine promiscuity received tacit social sanction. Today, women are no longer willing to accept "infidelity" as a man's privilege. They feel personally humiliated and either retaliate or consider an act of unfaithfulness as tantamount to putting an end to a marriage that otherwise may be healthy.

The terms "infidelity" and "cheating" need to be reevaluated in our present democratic setting. The philandering husband of yore did not consider himself to be "unfaithful" to his wife. He treated her respectfully, as the mistress of his household, as the mother of his children, as a social companion. His sexual escapades were considered to be a necessary outlet for his masculine needs. Women were supposed to have different needs; therefore, their sexual transgressions were not justifiable. Women, as the mothers, had to be chaste—so the dominant male society decreed. Women had to remain "faithful" and "clean"—otherwise, they had no right to any consideration and respect.

It is obvious that the requirement of faithfulness among women reflected male possessiveness. The husband "possessed" his wife, as one can own property and jewelry. But only as part of possessiveness has the term "infidelity" or "unfaithfulness" any significance. The wife of the past never "possessed" a husband. He owned her; therefore, his extramarital relations constituted neither unfaithfulness nor infidelity. Yet what constituted transgression or infidelity on her part depended on the state of subjugation in which she was held. Muslim women were unfaithful if they showed their faces to another man. In other countries, women were not permitted to go out in the street without a companion; a married woman was unfaithful if she as much as looked at a stranger. With the increase in their independence and freedom, women increasingly ventured out into the world by themselves as free agents. But still, the question remained unanswered as to what extent a married woman could go without becoming unfaithful.

Is it an act of unfaithfulness and infidelity if we go with a person of the opposite sex to lunch or dinner or to a movie? Or does it depend entirely on our feelings about that person? Then, is it no infidelity if we think romantically or sexually of another person or dream of him or are aroused by him? Is it infidelity to give a kiss or to hug, or is this state of unfaithfulness limited to physical contact beginning with holding hands? Is such contact only permissible at parties and not in private? Or does infidelity only involve sexual intercourse? To be sure, almost everybody has a definite idea about these questions, but his ideas may differ greatly with those of his neighbor.

A NEW SEXUAL CODE

It is obvious that our sexual code is no longer what it was, and many complain about immorality simply because few adhere to the code of the past.

The newly established equality between men and women confronts us with the task of determining a new sexual code, since the old pattern of double standards is no longer acceptable.

With the disintegration of traditional moral concepts, confusion sets in. Since the rigid sexual code of the past is rejected by many, and a new one not yet firmly established, everyone is not only free but also almost obliged to reach his own conclusions, to develop his own attitudes toward sex and about proper sexual conduct. Group identifications play an important part, but by no means diminish the confusion, since various cultural, racial, national, religious, and economic groups establish different patterns for themselves.

At any time we can distinguish three levels of sexual norms. There is first the *openly declared code*. Usually, this code conforms more or less to accepted religious and secular prescriptions. Monogamy is accepted, as a rule, and women are still considered in the same way as they have been throughout the ages; they are still expected to be chaste and faithful, and, for some people, virginity is still sacred. Even men who have doubts about these rigid demands usually do not fail to impose them on their own women: wives and daughters. A son is usually "excused" for what a daughter would never be permitted to do.

However, what people say about sex and propriety is not necessarily what they really consider to be right and wrong. The *private code* in which each one really believes is on the second level. And there is still a third level sexual code, namely, *actual practice*. Many do what they themselves consider to be wrong. Their actions are not in line with their value systems.

Kinsey did a disservice to the contemporary concept of sex. He mainly recorded what people actually did, giving the impression that, by their actions, they expressed their value systems. This is not correct. For instance, a girl may believe in "free love" but not practice it. Conversely, a boy who masturbates may not consider masturbation a "proper" thing to do. In other words, it is the *belief* that expresses moral codes, not the actions. Belief and conviction alone can form the basis of value judgment. Unfortunately, few realize what their own moral beliefs are and know even less about that of others. It is almost impossible at the present time to recognize any definite code of sexual behavior that would be acceptable to most people and represent contemporary conventions.

The absence of a well-defined set of sexual mores is particularly felt by the younger generation; few young people still accept unequivocably adult standards, particularly since they are fully cognizant of the many contradictions and uncertainties in the attitudes of adults toward sex. Young people want answers, but who is to give them answers?

One cannot predict the sexual code that eventually will emerge and be generally accepted. However, it is certain that women and children will play an important role in determining new sexual standards.

THE FUTURE OF MARRIAGE

Many people have questioned whether marriage as an institution will survive. Certainly marriage today no longer fulfills the three functions that it fulfilled throughout the ages. First, marriage was the basis for economic survival. Without a provider, the family could not exist. Today, many women are quite able to support a family without a husband. Second, only in marriage was sexual gratification permitted, at least for women, and a certain moral code did not permit extramarital relationships for men, either, unless they were "discreet." Today, sexual activity outside marriage is common. As far as the third marital function, that of raising children, is concerned, we find not only that many parents are presently ill-equipped to raise their children properly, but that many women raise their children without fathers.

A distressing fact that may contribute greatly to the growing doubt of the need for marriage is the increased availability of sexual gratification outside marriage. Many reasons are given for this development, the chief of which probably is that extramarital relationships allow unattended "time outs" away from the other partner and cut down on the pressures a couple face. But there are also the lure of the forbidden and the constant search for the new conquests.

Despite such developments, there can be little doubt that a marital union to which both partners give themselves totally, spiritually as well as physically, is still one of man's highest aspirations. Unfortunately, our inability to function as equals in close relationships impairs such a union. This is why sex continues to be a disturbing factor in marriage. However, we may assume that man, once he has learned to live as an equal among equals, will find monogamy the ideal institution because it will not be imposed upon him by pressure of society and maintained by law. Monogamy will be chosen because it satisfies deeper needs. It means partnership and sharing what may come for better or worse. Only then will sex lose its faculty of arousing anxiety, fear, and guilt feelings.

If fears—of failure, humiliation, censure, economic hardship, detrimental impact on the children—are absent, the sexual function will appear altogether in a different light. Impotence, frigidity, and homosexuality are consequences of such fears, materialized by anticipation. Possessiveness and jealousy, with their inevitable consequences—resentment and retribution—may become obsolete. Each one will be free to do what he decides since he respects the same rights of his spouse. The attraction that a spouse may feel for another person may be tolerated without resentment and fear. Sex will stop being sin, and the desire of the partners to belong to each other will preclude restrictions to each one's full freedom of movement. The real uniting force will be the decision to be and live with each other, regarding the other as part of one's life, independent of unavoidable emotional fluctuations. Marital partners do not have to regard each other as threats; both can contribute to the richness of their union.

THE ROLE OF THE PARENT

How does equality affect the father's function within the family? Obviously the effect is great because the strong father figure is mostly gone for good—and where it still exists, it exerts a dubious influence. The most capable and virile men often affect their children quite adversely. Their sons despair of their ability ever to be as strong and capable as their fathers; therefore they doubt their ability to be "real men." Daughters of strong men receive the picture of a superior man that few contemporary males can ever match. Neither realizes that the father is the last remnant of a vanishing masculine superior power.

Any assumption that a certain type of mother or father is necessary for the proper upbringing of children is fallacious. A parent who knows what to do with his children and how to influence them can be highly successful, regardless of his personality. A father who is interested in influencing his children can learn how to do that as well as can their mother. But one thing can never be done in a democracy: the father cannot tell the mother what to do, nor can she tell him. Neither has the power or authority to tell others what to do, but each has a full opportunity to exert his or her own beneficial influence.

The changing status of woman also involves a change in her role and function as a mother. The father, no longer universally recognized as the head of the family, is often replaced as such by the mother. As a consequence, he either withdraws from the task of raising children or opposes his wife in her methods. In any case, we can no longer say, "Father knows best,"—in most cases, Mother does!

The competitive atmosphere in the family affects the relationship between parents and children and between the children themselves. In a feudal family the firstborn son was supreme; no other child could challenge his superior status. Today each child fights for his own position against the rest, often siding with one parent against the other. We no longer find definite masculine and feminine patterns in the family. No longer is the masculine pattern of a family followed exclusively by boys. Girls may follow the traits of the father and boys those of the mother, resulting in mixtures and confusing patterns seldom found in a static social order where masculine superiority is well defined.[16]

Mothers pay a high price for the position they have obtained within the family. Their prestige becomes gravely involved when the children do not accept their authority and the rules they establish. Consequently, there is a growing sense of inadequacy among mothers. They take every act of misbehavior and every misdemeanor of their children as a sign of personal failure. The high moral and intellectual standards that many women have chosen as part of their striving for equality do not necessarily stimulate the children to emulation; rather, they inhibit them. Many ambitious and perfectionistic mothers discourage their husbands and children, who simply cannot live up to the expectations of their wives or mothers. Then the women are surprised and shocked by

16. In many Latin countries the old roles of masculinity-femininity are still in force, leading boys and girls into well-defined patterns of function and behavior.

inadequacies and failures, which they themselves have induced. An "efficient" mother is often the greatest obstacle to a child's development.

The greatest price is paid by such mothers when the children grow up. Then they lose their queenly status. When the children grow up, get married, and settle down, there is nothing left for the mother to do. The children remove themselves from her supervision and leave an emptiness in her life. The husband is often little involved with the children and when they leave, the mother no longer has any function in the family.

Herein lies the reason for many of the nervous breakdowns experienced by efficient mothers around the period of their climacterics. The "change of life" is less a change within the glandular system than a change in the social function of a woman. Any modern woman who devotes herself entirely to her family and to rearing children exposes herself to such a crisis.

Thus as women gain equality, they can no longer confine their functions to the family circle. Indeed, women who had been accustomed to studying and holding a job and who are suddenly thrust by marriage into the traditional roles of housewives find themselves at a loss when their function as mother has ended. They have either lost their occupational skills or failed to develop them sufficiently; therefore, they cannot find jobs that will give them status and responsibility equal to what they had enjoyed within their families. They have become mature and efficient, and they cannot start from scratch vocationally without losing prestige and significance.

MOTHERHOOD OR CAREER?

An important challenge for a modern woman, therefore, is to find a new equilibrium for herself between a career and motherhood. It is no longer possible to choose one course at the expense of the other. Many who have realized the full impact of our cultural development believe that a woman can—and even must—choose between career and family. But consider how silly it would be to tell a man that he would have to choose between a job and having a family.

Naturally, the responsibilities of a woman as a mother entails greater obligations in time and effort than are required from a father. But the discharge of her obligation as wife and mother does not require as much time as many women—or men—are inclined to believe.

Technical progress has made housekeeping less time-consuming than ever before, and a woman's domestic work load will decrease even further as housework is recognized by husband and wife to be a common task—an inevitable result of progressive equality between the sexes. And as housework ceases to be an inferior task assigned to the "inferior" sex, domestic help may once again be available in the form of professional workers instead of the servants traditionally held in low esteem.

In any case, the *length* of time a mother spends with her children is not important. What is important is *how* she spends it. It has been declared that the child needs the physical proximity of the mother to develop emotionally and socially. If great emphasis is placed on feeding, weaning, toilet training, and the gratification of instinctual needs, the time the mother spends with the baby naturally becomes all-important. But if, on the other hand, the importance of social relationships is recognized, a different picture evolves. Then it is no longer the *time* that counts in the relationship between mother and child but the *kind of relationship* she establishes. Moreover there is some evidence that women are better mothers if they also have outside activities and interests. When they devote all their time and energies to the child, they run the danger of being wholly dependent on the child for their value and significance, thus smothering the child with their expectations.

Part IV

MAN AND HIS UNIVERSE

CHAPTER 8

**Man's Sense of Biological,
Social, and Cosmic Inferiority**

As we have seen, in a democratic society a man cannot live
in peace either with himself or with others unless he knows
and feels that he *is* equal in human dignity and worth to
every other person. But does he? In spite of his desire to
be treated as an equal, man has encountered many experiences that seem to confirm his assumption of personal deficiency. Is this paradox real or illusory? On the personal
level we have seen that it is illusory. But what about at other
levels? We move in the biological, social, and cosmic spheres.
These dimensions of human existence are interwoven but
merit separate scrutiny.

MAN'S BIOLOGICAL INFERIORITY

Biologically, man is a creature of nature. He is a part of
it. Not only does nature surround him, but the forces of nature are at work within him, as in any plant or animal. Nevertheless, man is more than passive, submissive clay in nature's
hand. Man, too, is a creator, for he can change his own environment. Man, creator and creature, *interacts* with nature.
Discovering the laws of nature, man has utilized them to his
own advantage.

The limitations that nature imposes have not crushed man.
On the contrary, the struggle for survival prompted human
evolution and human progress. Nature is man's friend as well
as his enemy. It offers a constant threat of extinction, but it

also provides man with his natural potentialities for creation and growth. Nature has not endowed man with such aggressive weapons as claws, talons, and fangs, supported by powerful muscles. Nor has it armed him against attack with a shield like that of the turtle, lightness of foot like that of the deer, or protective coloration like that of fish and fowl. But nature has offered him successful compensations.

The physical weakness of man has been one of the paramount stimulations for the development of the human race. Man, physically weak in the face of many threats to his existence, eventually became the master of the elements and made nature bow to his will. Biologically man was inferior in all ordinary brute graces, but he compensated for his weakness by developing his intellect. Since he could not run fast and lacked aggressive strength, he developed the bow and arrow and eventually the spear. Since he was inadequately protected, he built shelters and used fur to keep himself warm. Through compensation for his biological inferiority, he gradually gained mastery over natural forces. He learned to put the elements in his service, and he made biology his partner in counteracting disease. Most recently his investigations have laid open the secrets of subatomic structure and shown the way to utilizing atomic energy.

Today man can claim many victories over the forces of nature. Science has given him the effective means to combat specific natural threats. It has provided new methods of investigation, research, and experimentation applicable to new predicaments as they arise. Physicians, for example, feel no panic at the appearance of a new disease. Rather, they face it with curiosity and attack it with determination. They do not feel insecure because of their human frailty or biological weakness. If they are overambitious, they may feel personally defeated if they lose one battle against death. But they do not consider mankind helpless and hopeless. They merely intensify their search with confidence that they, the representatives of mankind in the field of medicine, will eventually find a solution. Scientists in other fields react similarly when danger and possible catastrophe threaten. They study the new problem calmly and weigh tentative solutions. They are not alarmed by man's inadequacy; they are buttressed by his resources. Their trust in the efficacy of science fortifies them as might a layman's trust in religion.

Is man indeed frail in the face of natural forces? Not at all. All things considered, man has these forces well under control. Need we, for instance, fear fire? No—we understand its nature, know its utility, and put fire into our service. Considering the widespread use of the dangerous force of fire, catastrophies are relatively rare. Absolute biological security does not exist anywhere, but no one needs to live in constant fear.

Still, man's feeling of inferiority persists. The extent of his actual freedom from biological necessity is hardly recognized. Even scientists, succumbing to the lure of a defeatist philosophy, exaggerate the extent of man's biological weakness, saying that he is dominated by natural urges and animalistic instincts. Such theories express a deep doubt in man's adaptability to exert control over himself.

MAN'S SOCIAL INFERIORITY

The development of his brain and intellectual powers was only one of man's compensatory achievements. Another was the formation of closely knit social groups. Man has always lived a social existence. He is a socialized being. Whatever we call specifically human is an expression of social intercourse. Human qualities indicate each individual's social approaches, his methods of social participation, and his social interactions. Each man's personality is built on the concepts and attitudes that he has developed in his contact with others. The physical and mental constitution of man is adapted to social living.

The conflicts that seem to exist entirely within himself are really with people around him—with society and its agents.

The formation of groups, the establishment of close social contacts, and the emersion in a social atmosphere confront man with social laws that are at variance with the biological laws of nature.

When society is formed, a new dimension of organization is reached. Many contemporary scientists, particularly psychologists, ignore this new dimension and still tend to regard man as primarily a biological unit. Biological and social living are based on different premises and requirements. In a sense, social laws also are natural because the development of societies originated in the biological struggle for survival. Yet social living tends to modify the laws—"the laws of the jungle"—that characterize solitary living in nature.

Within society cooperation is the basic principle. Even outside society, wherever one being depends on another for his survival, cooperation is necessary, particularly between a mother and her young. Nature, sometimes outwardly peaceful and harmonious, is pervaded by destructiveness. Each creature lives at the expense of another, the stronger overpowering the weaker and feeding on it: "Race living at the expense of race," as Emerson put it. But social living alters this pattern. Despite exploitation of certain groups by others, the premise of every society is mutual aid, not exploitation. Within the cultural period of civilization, which forms only a small part of human history, some of the cooperative elements of primitive society were lost, but the cooperative principle was still recognized in religious and state laws, which at least controlled and limited mutual exploitation. No close living is possible without cooperation. This is also true for animals who live in groups. The closer the social contact, the more integrated the individual into the group, the more pronounced is the differentiation between the ways of social and solitary life.

The full impact of the social atmosphere upon the biological functions may be observed whenever individual specimens are closely integrated within the group. It is not mere coincidence that bees, living in one of the most closely knit societies ever observed, have gained complete control over their sexual function—even over the sexual role of the individual bee. The queen bee produces males and females almost at will simply by fertilizing one egg and not another. More remarkable is the fact that the bees can raise asexual offspring merely by restricting their diet.

Ants behave in a similar way. In contrast to free-living animals, which are very much driven by their sexual urges to maintain their species, bees and ants have amazing control over their sex functions. For bees and ants the interests of the hive and nest seem to be more important than individual survival. In the human species also, the formation of groups deeply affects the function of the individual.

Society, developed as a defense against the overwhelming power of nature, permits man a certain independence from natural forces, both within and without himself. The group safeguards him from external dangers. It stimulates the utilization of his powers of reason, planning, and creativity so that he can deal with the complexity of social interactions. Yet freedom from the universal servitude to nature has not provided man with any sense of security. This feeling of insecurity is partly the consequence of man's inability to understand that he has tremendous biological powers at his disposal. We still cling to the belief that we are slaves when we actually have become masters. In fact, what most hampers our sense of security in life is not the natural dangers to which we are exposed, but our inability to control man-made social forces. Though it is hard to believe, with his long history of social problems, man is still experimenting with society. How can this puzzling paradox be explained? Has there not been enough time for mankind to get socially adjusted? Was Freud perhaps right when he claimed that social living is against human nature because society denies man the gratification of his innermost desires and "needs"?

Society itself is not man's enemy; *present* society, however, does not meet man's social needs. Man's foremost desire, finding a safe place within the group, is thwarted by a social system that threatens everyone's status and social position. A stable social relationship can be based only on a relationship of social equals, and doubt in ourselves prevents almost all of us from feeling equal.

Just as feeling biologically inferior deprives man of his identification with life, so feeling socially inferior prevents man's participation in society with a sense of dignity and self-respect. Feelings of inferiority deprive him of a sense of belonging that alone can provide inner security.

MAN'S COSMIC INFERIORITY

During the evolution of the ancestral primate into *Homo sapiens,* with concomitant intellectual growth, man became aware of the vastness of the universe and of his own relative smallness. Here was new reason to feel inferior. Time and space became crushing realities, making the individual life span appear insignificantly small and the individual a negligible entity. The perception of the immense universe oppressed man with a sense of helplessness and personal insignificance. But again the characteristic dynamics of an inferiority feeling —a striving for compensation—came into play. Man began to look for his own spiritual survival—for life after death, for immortality. Philosophy, art, and religion stemmed from man's desire to compensate for his feeling of cosmic inferiority.

Man attempted to establish alliances with the powers of the beyond, to decipher eternal laws and esoteric and metaphysical principles. In his philosophy he matched wits with whatever powers ruled the universe. In his art he made himself a creator. In his religion he created divinities so that he could negotiate with them.

In another attempt to come to terms with the cosmos man set up a new deity—science—to provide a rational scheme for the mysteries that had always bewildered him. Empirical science promised to bring order into the chaos of life. It is true that science, so far, has only partly fulfilled its promise, but its failure to provide mankind with any lasting answers and solutions does not minimize the value of the scientific method, which helps us to understand that all truth is relative.

Here, then, is the inevitable challenge of the democratic evolution: man has to reconsider his position within the universe. Despite all of his limitations, man no longer needs to feel small and insignificant: he has a sure place everywhere as a biological, social, and spiritual being. Traditional patterns of thinking and feeling still block man's realization of his own strength, value, and significance. The impact of the social changes around him and of the new perspectives opened by science is slow to be perceived. It is not easy for us to look at life and at ourselves differently from the way in which we were trained and to which we have become so accustomed through the ages. There is much to be learned before we can become inwardly the free men that we have declared ourselves to be.

CHAPTER 9 · **Man and Nature**

Most people enjoy a high degree of biological security; yet
many live in fear—fear of life, of fate. Why does this fear continue to threaten mankind? A further examination of man's
biological role reveals that the inferiority feeling that has so
strongly affected man's history and evolution persists for psychological, not biological, reasons.

THE SIGNIFICANCE OF LIFE

We all assume that each of us is "confronted" by life in all
its splendor, as if life were something outside ourselves. We
stand in awe before a snow-capped mountain, a waterfall, a
sunset, a raging forest fire, a thunderstorm, the mystery and
majesty of the northern lights. Before such tremendous phenomena we feel small and shrunken. In our awe, we hardly
realize that all this majesty—this mystery, this almost unbelievable perfection and power—is at our disposal. This same
power lies in ourselves, in our own bodies and especially in
our own minds. Life has found its highest and most highly
developed expression in man. *All the grandeur, beauty, and
creativeness of nature is within each of us.*

Is it not incredible, then, that we should be unaware of
what we actually *are?* Whoever neglects to assess his resources
and emphasizes his deficiencies inevitably feels small and insignificant and develops a sense of isolation within a superior,
dominating world. Instead of recognizing our oneness with
nature and life, instead of rejoicing in this deep unity, our

eternal belonging, we make life appear distant, superior to us, and even perhaps hostile.

This error is dangerous; for our attitude—whatever it is—is a strong motivating force. A poor and mistaken attitude endangers peace with life and ultimately peace with oneself. The man who distrusts life must also distrust himself. Failing to realize the colossal power in himself, he feels threatened and helpless before hostile forces outside or within himself. Since each individual exerts a powerful and pervasive influence over his own mind and body, defeatism or pessimism endangers his well-being—even his health. From self-distrust and timorousness spring new difficulties, dangers, and maladaptations to life. Conversely, full realization of our natural powers and advantages permits us to use them fully and effectively.

THE SIGNIFICANCE OF DEATH

A mistaken concept of life as a threat is often accompanied by a similar misconception regarding death. Death is felt to be a sinister power, dark and ugly, *opposed* to life. Yet nothing could be more wrong. Death is not opposed to life; it is its *prerequisite*. Without death there would be no life. Life is a process of growing, renewal, creation and recreation, generation and multiplication. Without death none of these could take place. If everything existed forever, there could be no change; hence, no growth, no progress. The disappearance of a being makes way for a new being.

We find both cultural and individual reasons for the fear of death. In some cultures death symbolizes man's smallness and feebleness. Death is taken as evidence of man's insignificance. Prompted by such fearful implications men have turned from accepting death and have blinded themselves to its true character. With proper perspectives, however, men could perceive that they have a secure place on earth and rec-

ognize the limitations that death imposes on the individual
without losing sight of man's importance and significance.

The fear of death indicates rebellion. To try to justify our
objections, we rationalize: death is "unfair." Unfair to whom?
True, death is a hardship, but not for those who die, only for
those who survive. No one wants to lose someone he loves;
hence, the survivor feels deprived and resentful. He pro-
fesses to mourn the dead; actually, he bewails *his own* predicament. He feels cheated, as if he possessed a property title to
the deceased. And while he outwardly deplores the dead
man's fate, he is actually deploring his own fate, sometimes to
the point of seeking to join the beloved in death. In his al-
legiance to the dead, the survivor minimizes his responsibility
to those who live. Rebellion against "fate" springs from an
unwillingness to accept life as it is.

Others have violent fears of dying. Such people are usually
concerned with their own control; hence, they are fearful of
anything that may control *them*. They avoid whatever threatens their power and try desperately to defeat any force
stronger than theirs. Death is the only power they cannot successfully defy and cannot ultimately escape. Consequently,
they fear death more than anything else. Paradoxically, they
may commit suicide rather than submit to the inevitable approach of death: they try to cheat death and deprive it of its
power.

Others cannot bear the thought that life will go on when
they are gone. They are unwilling to leave the feast for others
to enjoy. They want to go on living because otherwise they
might miss something. The desire for eternal life may also
be a compensation for man's feeling of smallness and his realization of life's limitation. Belief in eternity, however, may not
involve any fear of death because it does not reflect antagonism to life.

In a deeper sense, death symbolizes life. Our attitudes

toward death—acceptance or denunciation—reveal our attitudes toward life. If we free ourselves of our antagonism to both death and life, we can realize that death is not necessarily terrible. Most people die without suffering. Of course, anything alive wants to live; intrinsic to life is the desire to grow, to develop, to continue. But life is struggle too—pain and torture—and death is a release.

Even though man is desirous of prolonging life to the utmost, he can still accept death as he accepts any other contingency of life. Death is the price many are willing to pay for accepting the tasks of life: they are willing to risk death for what they consider worthwhile and important to live for. In their actions they prove that, for them, death is only a part of life.

OUR SO-CALLED URGES

Our inclination to be overawed by man's biological inferiority is reinforced by some actual experiences. Natural drives and urges *seem* to compel us and to defy our efforts at control. Nowhere, for example, do we encounter the domination of inner forces as strongly as in sex. Nature has endowed all its creatures with the drives of hunger and sex; one for the preservation of the individual and the other for the preservation of the species.

Yet we can resist the force of hunger if we decide to do so. Voluntary starvation is not infrequent; it is employed by prisoners, political idealists, and even children to express defiance and exert pressure. And after a few days of abstinence the desire to eat all but ceases. To this extent we can free ourselves from the domination of natural forces within us.

The same emancipation is true in regard to sex, although few are aware of this fact. It is possible to lead a completely sexless life. However, man's ability to resist hunger is much more readily recognized in our culture than is his ability to forego sex, an assumption reinforced in recent times by the widespread influence of Freud's theories.

The assumed inability of man to control his biological sexual urge is actually an expression of deep-seated biological inferiority feelings. The sexual urge is considered a part of man's animal nature, which is supposedly in conflict with the social demands imposed on man. But such assumptions do not take into account the true nature of man. His sexual function is fundamentally different from that found in other mammals, except for those animals that live in groups—apes and monkeys—animals that are domesticated, and animals that are kept in captivity. Unlike their wild ancestors, males often follow the human pattern. As in the case of the bees, the influence of social living is evident in the sexual behavior of man, and social living entails considerable freedom from biological forces.

Naturally, the physiological mechanisms of copulation, fertilization, sensuous stimulation, and gratification are similar in man and animals. But animals function under compulsion and are subject to restrictions not encountered by humans. Among most wild animals copulation can occur only during a limited period when the female is in heat. Man, like apes and domesticated animals, knows no such restriction. He can be sexually aroused and gratified independently of the menstrual cycle of the female. This freedom of man is based on his increased independence from glandular or biological influences. He can be sexually stimulated before his sex glands have matured and after they have ceased to function. Even castration, if performed after maturity, does not preclude the ability to perform the normal sexual act.

The power of nature over free living animals is not only restrictive, limiting sex activities to a specific mating period; it is also compulsive. A male animal encountering a female in heat will not be deterred from the sex act. A rival may drive him away, but he will not leave on his own account. In contrast, human beings are under no such compulsion. They can defer or forego the sex act if aroused, and they can even resist being aroused. They can adapt themselves to any exigency and decide the course of their conduct, free from the dictates of nature. If they are afraid of sex or more interested in other aspects of life, they may choose celibacy. They regulate their sexual lives according to the exigencies of travel, the social dictates of monogamy, or other considerations for the welfare and interest of their mates.

There is a third distinction between man and beast to be noted—a difference in goals. The sole object in the sexual behavior of nongregarious animals is male–female copulation. In humans, however, the goals may vary. Sexual desire may be directed toward a member of the opposite sex, a member of the same sex, one's own body, an animate object, or an inanimate object. Human sex is polymorphous. The desire of the individual can be gratified by any object he may happen to desire. *Man* is the decisive force, not nature in him.

The assumption that we are helpless under sexual sway is an illusion, fostered to facilitate evasion. In setting up sex as our master, we renounce our own power in order to escape the full responsibility for our actions.

Those who think that the sexual urge rules man are likely also to postulate a conflict between sexual drive and social need. *Such conflict does not exist.* Anyone who lets his sexual desire lead to a violation or neglect of social demands also expresses anti-social attitudes in other areas. Disregard of, or rebellion against, social obligations often involves the use of sex as a decoy and a tool. The rebellion does not stem from frustrated and uncontrollable sex impulses; it is part of the whole personality structure. The pretense that man has compulsive sex needs usually conceals the real issues. Sex is subsidiary to social intentions.

In this era of rapid change, science cannot escape upheavals. The Copenhagen Agreement of 1927, which marked the beginning of a new scientific era, ended the one that began with Kepler, Newton, and Galileo and opened new perspectives, not only in theoretical physics, but in all sciences, leading to new ways of thinking and problem-solving. Unfortunately, these revolutionary changes have so far not reached the average college graduate, unless he has studied physics and chemistry. Yet there is one factor that the changes in theoretical physics and in the new aspects of social relationships have in common: absolutes are gone.

THE RELATIVITY OF FACTS

Until the last century, the universe had been presumed to consist of matter, primarily of inanimate and animate objects. Today the universe is viewed as consisting of energy, which under certain conditions appears as matter. The fundamental significance of this discovery is the fact that we do not know things as they are, but only as they appear to us.

Einstein's Theory of Relativity revolutionized our thinking. Absolutes lost their status as touchstones of truth. Truth is relative, depending on the observer, and is true *only* from *his* point of view. Conflicting statements that in an absolute system are mutually exclusive can now all be correct. And as Einstein's Theory of Relativity introduced revolutionary scientific thoughts by destroying the objectivity of time and space, so the Gravitational Theory of Relativity has affected a hardly less important revolution by destroying our belief in the reality of gravitation as a "force."

Scientific research must work within its natural limitations. Werner Heisenberg's Uncertainty Principle, formulated in 1927, established an inevitable inaccuracy in man's scientific observations. Heisenberg demonstrated that it is impossible to specify or determine simultaneously the position *and* the velocity of a particle—in this case an electron—as accurately as we would wish. It is possible to fix either of these quantities as precisely as *necessary,* but the greater the precision in one, the greater the inevitable lack of definiteness in the other. Because of the minute quantities usually involved, the Uncertainty Principle is of no consequence in our ordinary experience, but it is of great importance in atomic experiments and in its philosophical implications.

But knowledge, though never absolute and complete, can yet be trustworthy. *Limitations are not deficiencies but aspects of reality.* The possibility of omniscience, Laplace's dream of the eighteenth century, is shattered forever.[1] This does not necessitate a return to mysticism, the vagueness characteristic of the prescientific era. Limitations of knowledge have been *scientifically* established. The Uncertainty Principle is not a declaration of scientific bankruptcy, not a profession of ignorance. Our recognition that there are limitations to what can be known does not make us less secure in our knowledge; rather, it fortifies our new ideas of what knowledge is.

CAUSALITY OR INDETERMINISM

In this new view of the world mechanistic determinism is no longer accepted as absolute and all-inclusive. The Carte-

---

1. Laplace assumed that everybody who knew everything that goes on in the universe at any given time could predict everything that would ever happen. This would be true only if an absolute cause-and-effect relationship existed between all events.

sian principle of causation, on which our scientific edifice has previously rested, must now be reconsidered, a difficult task for the scientist and for the educated public alike. The scientific approach has been directed toward exploring natural forces in order to explain all observable events, a task that distinguishes scientific thinking from that of the mystic, who ascribes events to demonic influence or unverifiable mystical forces such as spirits or the evil eye. The scientist of the past could not accept the mystic's "explanations"; nor can today's. Observing events, earlier scientists looked for demonstrable energies and forces that "caused" them. The concept of causality is deterministic: a cause always has the same effect, other conditions being equal. A cause is definite, absolute, unquestionable, certain. In this sense, the causal principle supports the absolutist and mechanistic pattern of thinking characteristic of an authoritarian society; no freedom of choice is permissible or even imaginable.

The notion that a given effect is due to a given cause has been the very essence of the traditional scientific method. But today the mechanistic concept of life and the universe is slowly being discarded. "Statistical probability" is being substituted for the certainties of the causal principle. The modern physicist observes that when he shoots electrons in one direction, some deviate in an unpredictable manner, going far astray for no apparent reason. Nevertheless, the majority of electrons hit the target as expected. There is no certainty, but there is a high degree of statistical probability. Predictions are possible in regard to mass phenomena, but the course of the *individual* particle cannot be accurately predicted. For instance, nobody can explain why electrons in an atom may suddenly change their orbit around the nucleus. There seems to be a factor at work other than the general "cause" that is responsible for the action of large numbers.

The philosophical controversy about this phenomenon still rages among physicists. Some are inclined to speak about psychological qualities in energy; others oppose such an assumption. But one thing is sure: chance has been recognized as an integral part of natural process.

Those brought up in the tradition of mechanistic–deterministic thinking may find it difficult to accept or even to understand this new concept. To give an example from our human experience: the number of suicides in any city can be predicted fairly accurately for the coming year. Certain factors "determine" this figure. The suicide rate rises with the price of grain, for instance, and decreases during revolutions, wars, and times of national catastrophe. We can say that socioeconomic factors "cause" the increase or decrease in the percentage of suicides of a given population. But while we can predict the numbers, we cannot foretell whether any specific person will or will not commit suicide next year. However accurate our prediction about great numbers may be, we cannot claim any assurance of what will occur in an individual instance.

We are thus confronted with a new dynamic process: the "freedom" of the smallest unit, be it electron or human individual. Adler's indeterministic assumption that the individual had freedom to choose his own goals, frowned upon by scientists at the time, has found support from research in the most reliable field of science, physics.[2] Research has also confirmed another of Adler's basic assumptions, namely, that the creative ability in man is closely related to man's wholeness as an individual. Adler called his school of thought "Individual Psychology" to indicate that at the basis of his theories is the recognition of man as a total unit: the term "individual" is used, in this sense, as something that cannot be divided into parts, that is "indivisible."

The theory of the wholeness of the personality, widely ac-

---

2. See the pamphlet on "Teleological Mechanisms" (New York: New York Academy of Science, 1948).

cepted in theory, is still difficult to comprehend. Scientific clarification of the function of the whole—which is more than the sum of its parts—provides a new insight and explains man's freedom to decide his own actions. For this reason it may be advisable to describe here at greater length the theories of Smuts, who recognized new dynamics in the whole.[3]

HOLISM

The theory of holism makes the existence of "wholes" a fundamental feature of the world. It regards natural objects, both animate and inanimate, as wholes and not merely as assemblages of elements and parts. Because wholes are more than the sum of their parts, the mechanical putting together of their parts will not produce them or account for their character or behavior. So-called parts are in fact not real. Usually they are abstract and artificial distinctions; they do not properly or adequately express what has gone toward the making of the thing as a whole.

In the past the scientific method had been based on the analysis of bodies as composed of fairly constant elements or parts, the sum of which accounted for the behavior of the body or organism. In such a scheme, material structures determine the functions of living bodies, and even mind is explained by physical mechanisms and processes. Holism implies two great departures from this orthodox scientific scheme. First, holism holds that matter, life, and mind do not consist of fixed, constant, and unalterable elements. Second, the whole, which has hardly been so recognized, ap-

---

3. G. C. Smuts, *Holism and Evolution* (New York: Macmillan, 1926). The Greek word *Holos* means "whole." Scientific investigation toward an understanding of the significance of wholes has been carried out for a considerable time. Gestalt Psychology emphasized the totality of a being, the configuration or *Gestalt*, which has attributes transcending the sum of its parts.

pears now as an active factor, more important than its parts or its elements. The whole is creative. Smuts gives the following explanation for this creativeness:

> When parts form a whole, something arises which is more than the parts. In the moment the whole is formed, "more" arises from "less." *The making of wholes makes the universe creative.*

In the course of the history of the earth, the forms of life have progressed from the simplest and lowest organisms to the highly organized forms of today, culminating in the human personality. The older view maintained that evolution was mainly an unfolding of forms that were already inherent in the old forms. There was no place for a concept of creativeness; for, if the effect could never be more than the cause, there was no room left for a creative progression. However, discoveries in geology, paleontology, and embryology seem to indicate that the old *does* give rise to genuinely new forms, which cannot be reduced to the old and cannot be explained or accounted for by old forms alone. New species and races emerge through mutations, which form completely new organisms. The developments are creative acts of nature, which some mechanistic geneticists wish to attribute to the work of cosmic rays or similar yet unrecognized "forces."

The recognition of creative evolution reveals the traditional concept of "cause" as too abstractly and narrowly conceived; effect can and sometimes does transcend cause. Purely mechanical causation, which is perhaps a mere fiction, is *equative*, but holistic causation, which is the actual process, is *creative* and accounts for the advancement that actually occurs in nature.

The concept of the whole resolves the old controversy between freedom and determination in nature. The causal concept equates cause and effect and thus makes the cause determine the effect completely. If this causal concept is wrong, however, the concept of *necessity* has to be relinquished. If there is an undetermined creative element in the formation of wholes, not attributable to the conspiring causal elements, then there is *indetermination and freedom*. The creative element may be infinitesimally small and practically negligible in physical causation, because in physical causation we find relatively rigid mass phenomena; creativity is much more marked and appreciable in biological events; and it is still more so in the flexibility of mental processes. *Freedom thus becomes recognized as inherent in nature,* and the "quantity" of freedom increases with evolution, until on the human level it attains considerable dimension and becomes the basis for moral responsibility. In this way, freedom is recognized as a quality of the universe and not merely as an attribute of human will.

The old question of free will is thus seen in a new light. Scientists operating entirely on the principle of determinism denied free will, in opposition to the theologians who affirmed it. The latter asserted that man is fundamentally different from any other being, since he was created in the image of God. Only man had the knowledge of good and evil; he alone had the freedom to choose, the gift of free will. Today, self-determination can be accepted not only as a special quality of man but as a universal principle. Wherever there is a unit that functions as a whole, we find some independence from causal determining forces. Only when large numbers are involved can we speak about determinism; then the statistical probability of an effect gives the impression of causal determination.

REALITY AS INTERACTION

With the scientific endeavor to understand natural forces, we became aware that only rarely does one isolated force operate in any observable event. We were taught that an elec-

ept this new discovery of physical science, we
o recognize the power and influence of each i
s difficult to visualize that each of us possesses
strength, for we have been imbued for so l
ssumption of our own insignificance.

time has come to realize that we, influenced o
environmental social conditions, also influen
re is constant interaction. Our thoughts and actio
only the people around us, but through the
of others. This is one of the first lessons that ma
racy must learn, to become aware of his individu
e and strength.

recognized personal influence of the "little man
munity was dramatized in the movie, *It's a Won*
, which tells the story of an "insignificant" citizer
not advance himself and study because he had to
he small family store after his father's death. In-
nt his brother to school. He worked hard to make
hen, when he was "framed," he tried to kill him-
ent an angel to save him. The angel showed him
mmunity would have been like had he not lived.
ot realize how drastically he had influenced his
munity. Yet all he did was what you and I are
t everyone else would do. But except in a fairy
n never see the full impact of our endeavors.
o, had the help of a recording angel, we might be
t the influence we exert. Because what we do
gnificant, we can hardly imagine the extent to
deeds have affected people around us. An inci-
d may change the direction of a person's life;
m and through what he is doing someone else
uenced. By expressing our thoughts, our beliefs,
ns, we change the world around us.
y lives are fashioned by the social atmosphere in
ve, by conventions and values. At the same time,

tric current goes through the wire to light a lamp. This is a good example of the assumption of *one* cause—the difference of the potential between the positive and the negative poles—producing the electric current. Today we conceive of the electric current as the result of a great number of energy interchanges, taking place not *in* but *around* the connecting wire. The field *around* the wire is responsible for the transmission of electric energy; it may prohibit the flow of energy or even reverse it. In other words, one event can be understood only when one sees the *whole field* in which the event takes place. Scientific investigation, then, must be multidimensional.

Things are no longer as simple as they once appeared. Interaction is constant; nothing is isolated. Cause and effect are not always certain. Truth and falsehood are relative to situations. Everything is in change; nothing is definite. With the Greek philosopher Heraclitus we can say, "Everything is in a state of flux."

Different scientific investigations fortify this view of the relativity of facts. Korszybsky's *General Semantics* points to a new scientific flexibility in contrast to the rigidity of the Aristotelian doctrines of logic. The fact that every word used in everyday life has many shades of meaning reveals an unrecognized subjectivity in areas people believe to be objective and precise. We all use the same words, but we do not always mean the same thing. *General Semantics* emphasizes the faultiness of such an assumption. A great deal of previous certainty is taken away from us. We can no longer take things for granted. We must see them in all aspects, in the total situation, from all possible angles and dimensions.   —

The constant changes that go on in our ways of thinking and seeing can no longer be overlooked. Many may react to the fact of change with uneasiness and fear. Even among scientists we find revolt against the assumption of uncertainty as a universal principle, against the possibility that right and wrong are relative, that logical contradictions become irrelevant under certain circumstances. Many would like to maintain the status quo; they want security and fear change. They want to know where they stand, in simple, unmistakable terms. Science can no longer offer such security; on the contrary, it destroys cherished assumptions. Science provokes constant reexamination and reorientation.

But is it true that constant change must produce insecurity, that *absolute* values are necessary for orientation, that only the black-white picture of good and evil can provide signposts for proper conduct? Those who cannot swim may be alarmed at the prospect of finding themselves in deep water. But when they learn to swim, they move freely and securely in the new medium. *Their security lies within themselves. The only basis for security is the realization of one's own strength,* of one's ability to cope with whatever may arise. Then one can face all contingencies of life courageously, take in his stride whatever may come, and make the best of it.

Today more than ever we need a courageous attitude. The old signposts presented by dogmatic authority are crumbling. Man must learn to rely on himself in his interaction with his environment. He must discover his own strength and power. As our picture of the world changes, our concept of man changes. He is part of the universe, full of the same puzzles, contradictory tendencies, deceiving facets, and unpredictable creativity as the world around him.

CHAPTER 11 · **Man and**

We have been accustome
consequence of one specifi
ingly, the individual appea
which he lives. Social influe
by persons who control l
kings, political leaders, an
ences are almost insignifica
to an authoritarian society
as inferior, lacking intellige
rulers could know what wa
alone were blessed by divir
this light social adjustmen
conformity.

THE ST
INDIVIDU

It is more than incidenta
verse and the nature of ma
new concepts will have a p
our society. The nuclear p
been discovered at the s
glimpse of the intrinsic po
changes, both in science
they open new perspective
ence. Who could have sus
could yield such tremendo

tate to ac
still slow
vidual. It
mendous
with the a

Yet the
selves by
them. The
affect not
thousands
in a demo
importanc

This un
on his com
derful Lif
who could
take over
stead, he s
a living. T
self. God s
what his c
He did n
whole com
doing, wha
tale, we ca

If we, to
surprised
seems insi
which our
dental wor
through h
may be in
our opinio

Our dai
which we

our way of dealing with our problems affects the conditions and mores in our community. We either promote new standards or fortify old ones; we strengthen certain values in the community and weaken others. Our relationship to our families is by no means a private affair. Whether we spank our children or refrain from spanking them affects their friends and their friends' relationships to their parents. The atmosphere of the family is contagious. Our attitude at work makes its imprint on the whole organization, promotes or destroys morale and efficiency.

New discoveries in group dynamics indicate that the atmosphere and configuration of any group are influenced not only by the leader but by every one of its members. The power of the leader ends when he loses his followers. In a democratic atmosphere any effort to dominate the group is usually short-lived, for the little man counts and the leader must depend on him for support.

Society is not *imposed upon* individuals; it is *composed of* them. We tend to forget this because we underestimate our own social significance. We have the same mistaken attitude toward society as we have toward life: we consider both as if they were *outside* us, whereas actually both life and society are embodied *in* us. We *are* life and society. We think our neighbors can influence our lives, for better or for worse, but we are also our neighbors' neighbors. We are interdependent; each of us influences and is influenced.

WHAT IS "ADJUSTMENT"?

Interaction between the individual and society puts the question of social adjustment into a new light. If we do not recognize this interaction, we see social adjustment as simple and well defined, consisting of the desire and ability to conform, to behave in accordance with the demands of the group, to accept and submit to existing social laws and conventions.

In an autocratic society every individual had his specific
place by birth; he functioned within a well-defined field and
in a well-defined manner, because morals, values, and rules
for proper conduct were handed down to him from generation to generation. But in a mobile democratic society the
function and place of each individual is changeable. Each
man can move up or down the social ladder; each can enter
social groups with different values and mores. And each
group can determine its own conventions and values within
the general frame of our culture; consequently, we find that
there is a wide range of values within the social reach of each
individual. He can choose his own religious, political, and
social affiliations. Conformity to the ground rules of one
group does not mean conformity in another area. A child
may be fully conforming and therefore apparently well adjusted at home and still find it difficult to conform to the regulations of school or to the code of his peers. A laborer may be
considered well adjusted on the job, while his union colleagues may regard him, with justification, as disloyal. *Social
adjustment is no longer identical with conformity.*

Another factor complicates the problem of adjustment in a
democratic society. In a static, autocratic society changes took
place slowly. Changes in values, in conventions, and in mores
came gradually. Under such circumstances the individual
had little opportunity to take an active part in producing
change. Unless a man happened to live at a moment of crisis
and sudden change or belonged to a group that was involved
in stimulating such changes, his life span was embedded in a
set pattern. In contrast, our cultural era is characterized by
fast and far-reaching changes. The individual today has not
only the opportunity to take, but the responsibility for taking
an active part in shaping the world around him. His obligations to society include contributions to its improvement and
possible opposition to existing values and conventions. The
individual is living on two planes: within a community, with

its established standards and values; and within mankind, with its evolution toward new mores and values.

How can we adjust to both sets of demands when the two differ so often and so widely? Is it possible to be adjusted to one aspect and not to the other? Conforming to existing rules and conventions, we may easily become obstacles to change and progress. On the other hand, sincere concern with the need for improvement and progress may violate existing conventions and appear as maladjustment. The decision as to who is out of step depends on the trend of social evolution and the viewpoint of the observer. If the rebel fails, he is a criminal; if he succeeds, he becomes a hero.

We operate in a precarious equilibrium, exposed simultaneously to the pressure of the status quo and to the need for change and improvement. Yet a satisfactory resolution of these contradictory social demands, though difficult, is not impossible. In the general confusion of ideals, interests, and purposes two considerations may be valid. First, we need a clear perception of the trends of social evolution, so that we may know which deviations from the status quo are necessary and desirable. Second, we need to know the basic requirements for social participation and integration. Fulfilling these requirements in our contacts with people, we do not risk the danger of creating undue antagonism in the realization of our ideals. On the contrary, our ability to cooperate with others increases our chances of promoting improvements. In this way we can combine consideration for the needs of the group to which we belong with consideration for the future community we want to build.

THE DIRECTION OF SOCIAL EVOLUTION

The social changes that we are witnessing are often attributed to technical progress. True, science is transforming our world continuously and rapidly. The earth shrinks with each new development in transportation. The complexion of family life varies with the introduction of each new gadget—radio, television, frozen foods, mechanical household aids. The community is affected by medical progress through an increase in the proportion of older people and the decrease in the infant mortality rate. But this change in the physical makeup of our world is minute in comparison with the transformations that are occurring with increasing speed in the social order. The growing equality between men and women, the growing power of labor, the social claims of minority groups, and our acute awareness of our international interdependence are transforming our world within a generation.

This dual aspect of our evolution should keep us from overemphasizing the physical side of progress. The physical side is indeed important and should not be neglected. Better schools, better educational and recreational facilities, mental hygiene and prevention of disease, cultural projects, civic improvement, both in the aesthetic amelioration of the community and in the efficient management of its agencies, demand attention; for all these improvements reflect our concern with the common citizen, his dignity, and his right to a happy and full life. But these constitute only a superficial aspect of a more fundamental evolution. Preoccupation with immediate daily necessities should not prevent us from considering a more basic need of our times: to help ourselves and others to become *better human beings*.

The dream of fulfillment for mankind has prompted much of man's social evolution. Philosophers, founders of religions, and leaders of political movements have devoted themselves to defining this goal and the path to it. Without this dream of fulfillment we would have no democracy today. Desires and ideals are strong social forces. Belonging to a community involves more than joining a church and participating in social activities. It involves the obligation to think about the kind of community it should be, about how we can help one another, not only materially, not only through the development of institutions, but in the spirit, in the kind of relationships that we establish. Anyone who is concerned with the meaning of social evolution becomes a strong force for freedom, for right, for justice, for equality, for all the dreams of mankind that await fulfillment.

Of course, each of us has different ideas about the ways of achieving a peaceful, harmonious, and full life. In the past every conceivable method, including violence and warfare, has been used to impose ideals on others. Now the direction of evolution is becoming more clearly defined; it can provide a yardstick for evaluating ideals and endeavors. *The ideal of humanity is social equality.*

The knowledge that the relationship of equals is the *only* basis for harmonious and stable social living permits an evaluation of any step designed to bring about progress. Whatever promotes social equality is worthy of our support. We must oppose the pressure from those who fear change, partly because they do not know what to expect and partly because they benefit from the status quo of special privileges.

Our social attitudes—our concepts of humanity—are expressed through our actions. Belief or disbelief in the dignity of man determines our interactions with our children, with members of the opposite sex, with our friends and neighbors, with our superiors and subordinates. Unless we have grasped the significance of social equality, we cannot establish working relationships in our families, in our communities, or on our jobs. The promotion of social equality in our community is the most important task of our time.

PRINCIPLES OF SOCIAL PARTICIPATION

To achieve our ends we must first, as we have seen, be sure of our status as equals. Doubt of this would prevent us from treating others as equals.

Does our value depend only on what others may think of us, on how we measure up, on how much money we have? No. Such assumptions, though perpetrated by like-minded neighbors, are misleading. *By his mere existence each man already has a place.* We are all a part of our communities, regardless of the treatment we may receive from others. *Wherever a man is, he has a part;* he has a place, has rights and duties. Others may try to deny him the right to be here and may even try to impress upon him that he is not acceptable as a member of society. But this very interaction, regardless of how unpleasant and hostile it may be, proves that each of us is playing a role in our community. As long as we do not succumb to the efforts of others to make us feel inferior, as long as we are courageous enough to stand up for our rights, we can offset any effort to deprive us of our place. And in being courageous we serve not only our own interests but the best interests of the community.

Our sense of belonging cannot depend merely on what others feel about us because we can never hope to live in a community in which everybody is on our side. In the transitional world we inhabit, we cannot escape dislike, envy, disdain, antagonism, and hostility. At times these attitudes may be covered up by good manners; at other times they will break into the open. Making ourselves dependent on what others think, we sway like straws in the wind. Nobody can humiliate us as long as we do not feel humiliated.

To function in a social setting, we must know that *we belong* or we will not be able fully to participate in the give-and-take of social living. Every personal inadequacy and all destructive behavior can be traced to an *assumption* of having no value within the group. Conditioned throughout the thousands of years of social living, man is born with the potential of social interaction. A feeling of belonging is more important for his development than any gratification of so-called instinctual desires. No other hardship or misfortune can compare with the distress of losing status.

This has always been true. A feeling of belonging tied the individual to his surroundings when equality was no more than a dream. Undoubtedly, we can feel close to others without feeling equal to them. An overprotected child may feel very secure in his dependency on his loving mother. He may experience a subjective feeling of belonging despite—or perhaps because of—his smallness and helplessness. But today the child is no longer satisfied with mother's protection, for the day of protectors is gone. Before long, as we have seen, he will enslave his protector and use his smallness to tyrannize the strong. *The social atmosphere of democracy makes the assumption of equality essential for the development of a sense of belonging.* When the slaves in the South were freed, they missed the security of serfdom. They had to learn how to live as free men, and many—until recently—still preferred the protective domination of the South.

The need for recognition of each person as an equal is generally neglected. Our social atmosphere is competitive; one either feels inferior or struggles to protect an assumed superiority. Hence, we all live in a state of distance and defensiveness, even within our own families, and more so within our communities. Particularly among city-dwellers, social remoteness is the rule. Yet the modern world has seen a dramatic illustration of how unnecessary this state of individual defensiveness is, during the bombardment of London.

During World War II people lived under most trying and disastrous circumstances. When they left their homes in the morning, they did not know whether they would return, or, if they themselves survived, whether their belongings, friends, or relatives would. It was a time of utmost physical insecurity. Yet the spirit of the population was startling. A great number of people lived in a state of near elation, and there was little evidence of fear, apprehension, or resentment. What affected the population more than the impending danger was the experience of unexpected social closeness. In the bomb shelters all were alike, all equal. Differences in wealth, social position, individual skills, and status did not matter. For the first time in their lives these people experienced a social homogeneity that broke down the walls that had hitherto surrounded each individual and each family.

When people are thrown together in time of stress, they forget individual and social distinctions and experience a feeling of belonging that far outweighs the unpleasant and distressing nature of their common predicament. Conversely, when full social integration is impossible, rivalries outweigh real dangers and create more misery than any physical hardship can. *Social integration or the lack of it determines happiness or misery for each individual.*

Thus Dr. E. O. Lewis, president of the Section of Psychiatry of the Royal Society of Medicine, describes the extent and dangers of emotional isolation of the city population.

The great contrast between the social life in rural and urban communities is the degree of cohesiveness. In the country districts family bonds are strong, and the people know one another intimately, and usually are keenly interested in local affairs. The social life of our large towns is very different. The attitude of the average Londoner toward the people he meets every day can be appropriately described as mildly paranoidal. Neighbourliness is a lost art in our large towns. People live thirty or more years in the same house without taking the slightest interest in local affairs. If one may be pardoned a double literary lapse into paradox and hyperbole, the population of a dormitory suburb may be described as an amorphous agglomeration of unsociables.

Urbanization appears to be an inevitable concomitant of modern civilization; but the disintegration of social life in our large towns is inimical to political and cultural progress. Unfortunately, the mass entertainments of cinemas, wireless, and sports aggravate this tendency to social disintegration. . . . But a crowd is the antithesis of the real social group, where men and women meet in small numbers to discuss and exchange views on politics, local administration, education, music, and cultural subjects. These discussions enable men and women to understand one another's views and even if agreement is not reached, some common line of action on practical affairs is adopted. The decline of such groups in our large towns during the last few decades causes much concern to all social workers. *It is no exaggeration to state that the future of democracy depends largely upon a greater measure of social cohesiveness in our large towns.*[4]

As society is increasingly polarized into mutually antagonistic groups, the communities are often aroused as never before. Yet there is little combined action, and where there is, groups unite forces only to fight against something or someone. Each family is, in most cases, an isolated unit, often torn apart by the antagonisms within the family itself. The community *could* become the place where all divergent trends and antagonisms are discussed. In fact, the community is potentially the most powerful means for building a bridge of mutual understanding and cooperation on the basis of social equality.

SOCIAL EQUALITY

It is hard to believe that the idea of social equality is almost foreign to our thinking. This is paradoxical, since we in the United States have gained more equality than any other people in the world. As an example, nowhere else have women gained rights approaching those of men to the same extent, nor elsewhere can children claim the privileges that are granted them in America. Yet the possibility that every

---

4. *Proceedings of the Royal Society of Medicine,* Vol. 44, 1951, p. 117.

individual can have the same social status is abhorrent to many Americans. They cannot grasp the meaning of social equality, which for them is a vague or entirely rejected concept.

This peculiar state of affairs can perhaps be explained by looking briefly at American history. One of the first social analysts of the American Revolution, De Tocqueville, considered the "equality principle" as the most outstanding feature of American democracy. How then did it later disappear from the American scene? In the reactionary period around 1800, under the influence of Hamilton and Adams, the wealthy landowners rebelled against the growing rights of the uneducated masses. They decried the term "democracy" and preferred to speak of the United States as a "republic." At that time the term "equality" was replaced by the doctrine of "equal opportunity," which has been maintained throughout the years.

The struggle to minimize the significance of equality was clearly evidenced in the changes that Jefferson was forced to make in his formulation of the Declaration of Independence. In his original draft, he not only stated that "All men are created equal"; he continued: "from that equal creation, they derive rights inherent and inalienable." This section he had to remove in later drafts. We are made to believe that we are *created* equal, but that from then on we are no longer equal. Only those who make use of their opportunities and develop special traits and skills can be assured of their value; those who do not take advantage of their opportunities fall by the wayside. All that the Declaration of Independence leaves them are "certain inalienable rights": "life, liberty and the pursuit of happiness." The inherent rights derived from their equal creation are no longer mentioned. The formulation of "equal opportunity" soothes the conscience of those who still "believe in" equality and talk about it but have not the slightest idea what it means.

Actually, even equal opportunity has never existed: opportunities have always varied with family background. Moreover, even if we were able to provide each child with identical educational facilities and every citizen with the same chances for employment, opportunities would still not be equal. It is obvious that children of the same family do not have the same opportunities, for various reasons inherent in the dynamics within the family group. The concept of equal opportunity is fundamentally fallacious; it does not embody—rather it denies—the realization of basic social equality. As long as this ideal of equal opportunity is used as a substitute for true human equality, progress is retarded because the concept misleads our efforts.

Equal opportunity not only is a poor substitute for equality, it actually negates it. Thus Raymond Aron says:

> The more a society is imbued with the competitive spirit, the more it admits of inequality among individuals. Western society takes a sporting attitude toward equality: Let everyone begin at the same starting line, and may the best man win.[5]

John H. Schaar expresses the same sentiments:

> The equal opportunity principle is widely praised as an authentic expression of the democratic ideal and temper. . . . it is a cruel debasement of a genuinely democratic understanding of equality. The doctrine of equality of opportunity is the product of a competitive and fragmented society . . . It extends the market place mentality to all the spheres of life.
>
> The idea of equality of opportunity, whereas it seems to defend equality, really only defends the equal right to become unequal by competing against one's fellow. Hence, far from bringing men together, the equal-opportunity doctrine sets them against each other.[6]

---

5. Raymond Aron, *Progress and Disillusion: The Dialectic of Modern Society* (New York: Frederick A. Praeger, Inc., 1968).
6. John H. Schaar, "Equality of Opportunity and Beyond," in *Equality*, J. R. Pennock and J. W. Chapman, eds. (New York: Atherton Press, 1967).

The concepts of equality and of democracy, although widely used and acclaimed, are hardly understood and are difficult to accept and to put into practice. It seems to many that equality can never be achieved, that it is against human nature; inequality is regarded as part of social living. And there is some justification for this assumption. The history of mankind is replete with all kinds of social inequalities.

However, the strife for an egalitarian society expresses man's desire for social harmony, which has never before existed. The first development of democracy occurred in Greece, possibly through the influence of Buddhism. Democracy, the rule of the people, replaced oligarchy, the rule of the few, and the Greek Stoics said that democracy required the recognition of human equality. It is true that the Greeks failed to give equal status to all: they limited equality to men and citizens; women and slaves were excluded. But Solon of Athens, for example, restricted the display of wealth to counteract an assumption of superiority and exhibited the qualities of democratic leadership by his genius for reconciling differences, taking the part of neither the rich nor the poor. He maintained that equality breeds no revolution.

The influence of the Greek Stoics reached Rome, and the Roman Stoics applied equality to law. For the first time, equality was put into practice: every Roman citizen was equal before the law. Under the influence of the Greek Stoics, early Christians created the first egalitarian societies in their communities.

But while the idea of equality spread throughout the whole cultural sphere, it did not last. In the fifth century the Augustinian doctrine of predestination replaced the Stoic-Christian ideas of the equality of man and gave rise to medieval orthodoxy. According to medieval thought, worldly inequality was a part of the divine scheme of things and the consequence of man's fall from grace, which was willed by God. The Roman and Byzantine cultures were destroyed by the barbarians, and the short democratic era gave way to the Dark Ages of feudalism.

The democratic trend, rekindled in the Renaissance, eventually led to the French, American, and Russian revolutions, which gave increased importance to equality and the rights of man, and reached its peak after World War II in the United States and in Israel.

Our present predicament arises from the fact that while we all have legally become equals, we do not know how to deal with each other as equals. Social equality is characterized by the unwillingness of anyone to submit to dictates. But instead of creating more harmony, the state of legal equality has intensified the war between all previously dominant and submissive groups. Still, we cannot turn the clock of time back; we have to go through the phase of the birthpains of a new society. *There are no ills created by democracy that cannot be cured by more democracy.* The spread of revolutions throughout the world has often been compared to the revolutions that shook Europe in 1848. At that time people were striving for their political freedom; today they strive for *participation in decision-making.*

While the turmoil within our present society is obvious, few realize the nature of the conflict. Negroes fight for civil rights, labor and women rebel, and children and youth are involved in the warfare of generations. Each group considers its case to be special. And few, like Aron, realize the universality of the conflict:

Adolescents do not refuse to listen to the advice of an elder, but they no longer obey the orders of the old. Women demand *true,* not theoretical equality. Just as American Negroes believe that separation is incompatible with equality, so women no longer accept a division of labor which would deprive them of full and complete participation in professional and civic affairs. They are no longer willing to devote themselves, as if this were their natural destiny, to the care of household and children.[7]

Aron raises the question: "Must we conclude that in the last analysis the insurmountable obstacle to equality is the very nature of social man?" And he answers: "We shall content ourselves with saying that the social order will achieve peace when the desire for distinction and prestige finds expression in nothing more harmful than snobbery."

But here I cannot agree with him. Intellectual and moral snobbism is more harmful than many realize. It hinders the rehabilitation of all who are deficient. The crucial point is the inability—or shall we say, the unwillingness—of most social scientists to accept a state of affairs in which their own superiority would be threatened.

A typical example is provided by Wilson. In order to reject the term equality, Wilson utterly confuses the issue.

> We have before us, it seems, a number of interlocking ideas, closely related to each other, yet perhaps distinguishable; and it is not clear just which ideas are normally or most usefully expressed by the word "equality." Concepts like equality, liberty and democracy are not ultimately defensible at all.

But then he makes it clear how easily one can understand and accept inequality. He gives the example of the inequality between the sexes:

> Female emancipation is an eccentricity, almost wholly confined to modern technological societies. Elsewhere it has generally been held that women, though undoubtedly superior to children, animals and furniture, should for some purposes be classified with them and not with men. They might have rights, but they were not equals. . . .
> Though women in our society may be emancipated in the

---

7. Aron, *Progress and Disillusion.*

sense of having the vote, being equal with men in the eyes of the law, being allowed to own property, take up careers and so forth, most honest men will admit that they are not psychologically emancipated. They do not desire to be treated as equals. In the last resort, they want the wills of men—or of a particular man—to count for more than their own. They may wish to be treated with respect, valued, loved and cherished, and deferred to on occasion; but they do not want an equal voice in decision making. Nor is it clear that men wish to give them an equal voice.[8]

Wilson may be right: many women behave as he indicates because they have not freed themselves from a slave mentality. But he himself is a victim of the same slave mentality, having no confidence in people, especially in women.

McKeon realizes that one great danger to equality lies in those who refute the very idea of equality.

We are in danger of forgetting what equality has come to mean in the centuries of discussion of its meaning. And we are in danger of losing the equalities which we have achieved during the centuries of struggle for equality. We have forgotten the meaning of equality to such an extent that reputable scientists devote ingenuity and scientific erudition to demonstrate that men are unequal. We have lost the moral motivation toward equality by supposing that equality is at best an effective though deceptive catch-phrase or by excusing inaction because the times or the circumstances are not right to put equality into effect.[9]

Johnson opposes the above sentiments:

When the basis for equality is sought in the realm of fact, the results are so markedly negative as to occasion wonder that

8. John Wilson, *Equality* (London: Hutchinson, 1966).
9. Richard McKeon, "The Practical Use of a Philosophy of Equality," in *Aspects of Human Equality*, L. Bryson et alia, eds. (New York: Harper & Row, 1957).

scholarly inquirers have so far persisted in the quest. . . . The ultimate test of democracy is the ability of the people as a whole to discover an authentic aristocracy of ability and character. The quest of human equality in a factual sense becomes more disappointing the further it is pursued.[10]

Other scientists also deny the possibility of human equality. The well-known psychologist B. F. Skinner, for example, has said:

> The central tradition of western thought which has cherished the essential dignity and liberty of the individual is, quite simply, no longer tenable in the face of modern scientific knowledge of the nature of man. . . . The individual is not responsible for what he does and it is useless to praise or blame him. Such a scientific view is distasteful to most of those who have been strongly affected by democratic philosophies.[11]

William G. Sumner heartily detested and excoriated the emphasis on equality, opportunity, and the rights of man. "The desire for equality was a superstitious yearning," he said.[12]

The predicament in which we find ourselves—the need to adjust to a new era of freedom—is not new. The same situation happened 3,500 years ago when Moses led the children of Israel out of Egypt from slavery into a free land. But neither Moses nor anyone else who had lived under slavery was permitted to enter the promised land; after 40 years of wandering in the desert everyone who had been a slave was dead. In contrast, we have to create a new society while many around us deny that it can be done. And we cannot wait until they all have died.

---

10. Ernest Johnson, "The Concept of Human Equality."
11. B. F. Skinner, *The Behavior of Organisms* (New York: Appleton-Century, 1938).
12. William G. Sumner, *The Science of Society* (New Haven, Conn.: Yale University Press, 1927).

Most Americans would consider it axiomatic that there should be equality before the law. But is that possible? Aron expresses the contemporary confusion. He realizes that "juridical equality is nothing without economic and social equality."[13] But he does not believe that social equality is possible.

We are confronted with the question of equality of social status—*social equality*. Can it be achieved or is it against human nature? I contend that inequality is arbitrary and against human nature, although a class and caste society has existed throughout our civilization. Moreover, the arbitrary nature of the imposed distinction is demonstrated by the changes that have taken place in the "qualifications" for superiority.

For a long time in man's history, the only basis for superiority was birth. A person was born high or low, and this decided his status. If one was born high, as a member of the aristocracy, one had to be treated with reverence, irrespective of any personal qualities. If one was born low, one had to be humble. This was true until feudalism ended. Does the fact that this superiority by birth existed for hundreds of years prove that it was "natural"? Recent developments have shown that the distinction was as arbitrary as any other form of superiority. And with the breakdown of feudal society, all other forms of superiority gradually became obsolete, too. We no longer recognize the superiority of nobility. Titles are no longer revered; their bearers often do not use them.

Then came the superiority of money. Everybody was worth as much as his bank account. The Depression took care of that. High esteem for the rich is waning. The same decline happened to masculine superiority. There are still some who believe in it, but their number is dwindling. We may well say that the traditionally inferior status of Negroes also is gone for good; they *no longer accept* white supremacy.

---

13. Aron, *Progress and Disillusion.*

We might assume that the present disregard for so many previous forms of dominance and superiority should open our eyes to the fallacy of the idea that any *individual* quality can provide superiority. Far from it. People are looking for a new yardstick to measure social status—and they have found one, at least for the moment: moral and intellectual superiority. Yet we may also assume that this form of newly won superiority will go the way of all the other transitory forms.

The danger of competition, providing the basis for personal superiority, is also becoming increasingly recognized, even though in the past competition was a necessary requirement for social mobility. The end of feudalism gave each individual a chance to climb as high as he could. Personal competition was inevitable. Much progress was achieved through competition, so that many cannot believe that people will do their best without competition. It is characteristic of our society that everyone tries to elevate himself, moving on a *vertical* plane,[14] out of fear that if he cannot be superior to others he will be lost and will be a failure. But social competition has outlived its usefulness. It pitches man against man, penetrating every family. The closer men live to each other, the more they compete. Brotherly love was once a symbol of great devotion; today we would not wish our worst enemies to be treated as brothers treat each other, each one looking only for his own advantage.

One of the reasons for the difficulty in recognizing the danger of competition and eliminating it is the lack of information on how and with what competition can be replaced. We have ample evidence that both the family and the school can operate much more harmoniously and effectively when competitive strife is replaced by cooperation. Growth and achievement can be obtained when everyone works toward a common

---

14. Lydia Sicher, "Education for Freedom," *American Journal of Individual Psychology,* Vol. 11, 1955, pp. 97-103.

goal, moving on a horizontal plane, growing through the desire to contribute, to experiment, to expand, without competing with anyone. This is how young children learn before they go to school, enjoying what they are doing without the anxiety and the fear of failure that characterize most classroom activities.

One might well ask if it is right to induce children not to compete with each other, since they sooner or later have to enter the highly competitive climate in our communities. The fact is that the *less* competitive a person is, the *better* he can stand up under competition. Such a person is not concerned with what others are doing, only with what he can do. The highly competitive person can stand competition only if he wins; he is vulnerable to every defeat. Parents and teachers can, if they want to, establish a cooperative atmosphere; yet most parents play one child against the other, making the good one better and the bad one worse. If the parents would put an end to this competitive strife, they would actually bring about a situation where each child is "his brother's keeper."

Before long the mad rush toward self-elevation will be recognized not only as a threat to the sanity and inner equilibrium of the individual but as the cause of failure and defeat. Everyone tries to find his place in life through achievement and possessions. A person may gain success, power, money, and love, but he will never achieve inner security thereby. Whatever he has will not be enough; or he may lose what he gained. And many people who do not achieve anything worthwhile give up in despair. No one can feel secure through whatever he may achieve or get; unless he realizes that he has a place by *his mere existence,* he will never find security.

Affected by slave mentalities, we believe that we must hold the whip over others and ourselves. We threaten, frighten, and discourage each other. In fact, if we are not satisfied with

ourselves as we are, the chances are that we never will be.
Only if we can make peace with ourselves and have the courage to be imperfect can we really progress.

Mary was a wonderful preacher. She spoke with the tongue
of angels, and people came from far and wide to listen to her.
One day a friend asked her: "Mary, how did you become such
a wonderful preacher?" She thought for a moment and then
said: "Frankly, I don't know. I only know that I was visited
by the devil after each sermon. One day he came and gave me
a pat on the shoulder, saying how wonderful the sermon was.
The next time he gave me a kick because my sermon was so
poor, and each time I had to fight off the devil. And since he
no longer comes to visit me I think I am doing all right."

Mary realized the devil of vanity. She, like so many of us,
worshiped the Golden Calf of personal success. But when we
are no longer concerned with success, we lose the fear of failure.

Wherever we are and whatever we do, we are part of life, of
the community. Generations come and go. Today we are on
the stage of life. Each generation and each one of us makes his
contribution, makes life around him better or worse, promotes progress or prevents it. Our function is not to prove
how good we are but to show what we can contribute to the
welfare of others. We are all part of an orchestra in which
each player has his part, big or small.

WHAT IS DEMOCRACY?

It is strange that the question of the definition of democracy is ever raised. Don't we all believe in democracy, in the
democratic process? We even go so far, as Americans, to try to
export our concept of democracy to the rest of the world,
without even being very clear about what it is. If our ideas of
democracy were clear, we would not have such a wide range
of often contradictory opinions.

The term "democracy" has been primarily used—and still is used by many today—to mean government by the people, who exercise their rule through their representatives. But democracy is obviously more than that: it concerns the rights of people. Many people believe that democracy gives everyone the freedom to do what he wants, provided he does no harm to anyone else. Kant, for example, considered that "Everyone is entitled to seek his own happiness in the way that seems to him best, if he does not infringe the liberty of others in striving after a similar help for themselves."[15] Similar ideas are expressed by Herbert Spencer: "Every man is free to do that which he wills, provided he infringes not the equal freedom of any other man."[16]

Many share these sentiments. But we do not become democratic merely by stopping being autocratic. The collapse of autocracy may as easily lead to anarchy unless appropriate steps are taken. Indeed, the constant shifting from the autocratic approach to the permissive is part of our dilemma in defining democracy.

Democracy is concerned with fundamental human rights. And these rights are based on the recognition of the equality of all citizens. Certain aspects of equality have been discussed previously; others are easily acceptable; still others are misunderstood or even rejected, with damaging effects on the democratic process.

Many people consider the term democracy ambiguous. Frondizi describes the situation:

> The word democracy has been used and is still used with a
> great variety of meanings, some of them incompatible with each
> other. Pages after pages can be filled with quotations, giving
> evidence to the divergent views of the word . . . The word de-

---

15. Immanuel Kant, *Principles of Politics* (Edinburgh: Clark, 1891).
16. Herbert Spencer in *Political Justice*, R. B. Brant, ed. (Englewood, N.J.: Prentice-Hall, 1962).

mocracy is neither ambiguous nor unambiguous per se. The ambiguity depends upon its usage. Its ambiguous or precise meaning depends on how we use it or the way we define it.[17]

Such "misunderstandings" are not incidental. On the one hand, each has the right to define democracy in his own way, so that almost everybody today feels justified in calling himself democratic and progressive, although he may be the worst autocrat and oppose any idea of equality. Laswell expresses the ideas of those who are opposed to democracy, among them many psychoanalysts and behavioral scientists:

> Underlying the failure of the democratic dialogue is a more fundamental malaise, the democratic man. The individual is a poor judge of his own interest. Promoting discussion amongst all interests concerned frequently complicates social difficulties, for the discussion by far-flung interests arouses a psychology of conflict, which produces obstructive, fictitious and irrelevant values. Our thinking has too long been misled by the threadbare terminology of democracy versus dictatorship, of democracy versus aristocracy. We ought to be ruled by those best equipped to discern the truth and to administer harmonious relations, namely the social administrator and social scientist.[18]

One cause for confusion about equality is the different meanings applied to the term. In other languages, different words are used to define the different meanings of the word. For example, the Germans distinguish two meanings, *Gleichberechtigung* and *Gleichwertigheit,* which mean equal rights and equal worth, respectively. The concept of equal rights is generally accepted, but the assumption of equal worth for everyone meets opposition. The French also use two terms,

---

17. Risieri Frondizi in *Democracy in a World of Tensions,* R. McKeon, ed. (Chicago: University of Chicago Press, 1951).
18. Harold D. Laswell, *The Analysis of Political Behaviour* (London: Rutledge & Kegan Paul, 1948).

but their distinction between two fundamental kinds of equality is quite different. They speak about *égalité de droit* and *égalité de fait,* legal and practical equality, or equality in theory and practice.

Many believe firmly that to aim for equality of worth—true democracy—is an impossible goal since such equality has never been witnessed before. But it *did* happen. The early Christians and many other religious groups practiced equality. Occasionally there have been reports of groups that seemed to have had real social equality. Among the five primitive groups Margaret Mead examined in the South Sea Islands, one tribe in New Guinea, the Arapesh, achieved a remarkable degree of equality. The Arapesh have no gerontocracy of the kind found in many primitive societies, where the old dominate the young. They ignore the social significance of age by addressing a person as grandfather, brother, or son, notwithstanding his age. They do not attribute superiority to men or women, but let them share to an amazing degree responsibility and function. In raising their children they use neither reward nor punishment. They apparently have succeeded in building a community based on mutual respect, cooperation, trust, and consideration for all.[19]

THE DEMOCRATIC PROCESS

The constitution of a democratic country usually includes provisions for equal political rights and equal representation. But this ideal procedure has not been applied anywhere. Why?

The Marxists have a simple reply. They suggest that as long as there is economic inequality, those who wield economic power will prevent equal representation and equal voice, and that if the capitalistic system is replaced by social-

19. Margaret Mead, *From the South Seas.*

ism, true political democracy can be established. Yet communist states that claim to be democratic are autocratic regimes that deny each citizen political freedom.

Neither *political* nor *economic* equality is possible as long as there is no *social* equality. Only when all members of society are recognized and treated as equals can political, economic, and social harmony be established. The alternative is the continuation of the present war between all groups who fight for their rights *ad infinitum*.

The problem becomes obvious when we attempt to apply the democratic principle to all areas of human relations. The "democratic way" pertains to many aspects of social living and is used to describe specific forms of interpersonal and intergroup processes. In the area of interpersonal relationships confusion reigns, despite all the studies in political and behavioral sciences. Obviously, mistaken concepts exert their detrimental influence. Our difficulties arise from the fact that we do not know how to live with each other as equals. We need new techniques and approaches—in the family, in the schools, in the community, in industry, and in politics.

We are still saddled with an autocratic tradition and we still fail when we try to emancipate ourselves. In the ensuing confusion we do not realize our ability to create various kinds of social climates, some conducive to democratic procedures, others impeding or obstructing them.

Kurt Lewin demonstrated this in his Iowa Experiments, which are of crucial significance for our present predicament: he experimented with three different "social climates" in boys' clubs. He trained the leaders in three basic approaches: autocracy, democracy, and *laissez-faire* anarchy. The autocratic leader told the boys what to do; the democratic leader helped them to design and carry out projects; and the *laissez-faire* leader let the boys do what they wanted. The results are of profound importance. The autocratic and the democratic groups performed equally well, while the *laissez-faire* group did not produce anything.[20]

Clearly, the experiment points out several lessons. First, democracy should not be confused with anarchy.

The second important fact involves the differences in the activities of the boys. The autocratically governed group could work only when the leader was present. Otherwise they fought among themselves. They could function only under control. In contrast, the democratically led group continued their work when the leader was absent and got along with each other. They had an inner control.

The most striking and significant observation was made when the leader changed his role. When the democratic leader became autocratic, nothing happened. He had won the confidence of the boys; they went along with him, and in a short period of time they acted like the autocratically led group. But what happened when the autocratic leader was told to become democratic? Bedlam broke loose. It took the leader about a week before the boys settled down and became a democratic group.

When the autocratic pressure on a group stops, anarchy results. People become free to do what they want, without the necessary sense of responsibility. In the case of Lewin's boys, they had a leader who helped them to become democratic. In our society we do not have such leaders. Consequently, children as well as adults often abuse the freedom that the democratic evolution has provided for them. This is the dilemma of our time.

---

20. K. Lewin, R. Lippitt, and R. K. White, "Patterns of Aggressive Behavior in Experimentally Created Social Climates," *Journal of Social Psychology*, Vol. 10, 1939, pp. 271-299.

Part V

CONFLICTS AND THEIR SOLUTIONS

CHAPTER 12 · **The Process of Polarization**

Our cultural atmosphere is characterized by the abuse of democratic freedom. Society is torn apart; everyone considers his own rights and disregards the rights of others. The democratic freedom of everyone to do as he pleases accentuates the differences between the various race, sex, and age factions. This mutual antagonism is now called polarization.

A DIVIDED COMMUNITY

Various segments of the population have now created a common enemy: the "Establishment." The amazing fact is that everyone has a different notion about the nature of the Establishment. For the Negroes the Establishment is white racist; for women, patriarchal; for labor, exploitive; for children, adult. Many individuals belong to groups that others consider the Establishment, and many, in turn, fight their own brand of Establishment. Instead of consolidating their struggle against injustice, domination, and deprivation of rights, each group fights its own battle. And the fight is often very brutal.

Those in authority cannot understand this. They do not realize that there is a civil war going on, a war that justifies killing the enemy. Vietnam contributed its share to the ideology that the enemy can be fought with every conceivable method; the war in Vietnam triggered domestic antagonism against the authorities. But were it not for the Vietnam war, other justifications for the domestic warfare would be found.

We are on a collision course, and since nobody seems to know how to resolve the conflicts, we are in grave danger.

In the United States the most intensive civil strife involves blacks and whites. A close and inextricably entwined revolt is the rebellion of students and other groups who fight society. The economically deprived, criminals—even prisoners in jail—demand to be treated with respect. And each group that complains about the unfairness and the oppression of the Establishment does its best to provoke the Establishment. We live under the illusion that only through strife—often violent strife—can any progress be achieved. There is no doubt that some improvement can be obtained in this way, but at what price? The fight will go on and become more intense until methods to solve conflicts in a democratic way are known and applied.

Another form of polarization is also taking place: between those who call for law and order, hoping to suppress the rebellion with power, and those who side with the underprivileged and openly or tacitly support their rebellion. But neither method will bring about a solution of the conflicts. There will be no *law* and *order* until we have *peace* and *order* in our communities. As long as authorities delude themselves that they can establish order through oppression, they will only stimulate more rebellion. Violence and destruction will not be prevented by threats or by equally brutal acts of retaliation. New methods must be used to make the resort to violence unnecessary and useless, both for the offenders and the law enforcement agents.

One of the stumbling blocks for a new society is our criminal code. The code operates under the assumption that punishment can be effective and preventive. Most students of the law recognize this fallacy, but society still seems to be unwilling to give up the demand that the "punishment should fit the crime." Our penal institutions usually provide training for criminal careers. Jails are the breeding places for more crime, and the situation is worsened by the inhuman conditions found in many jails, to which even juvenile offenders are exposed.

Those who violate the law need *rehabilitation,* and punishment will never rehabilitate. There are better ways of treating criminals, and in some institutions a process of rehabilitation has already been established. Prisoners participate in decision-making and reexamine and change their values in group discussions. But the majority of our contemporaries consider this "coddling" the offenders.

The punitive spirit is evidenced by the way offenders are treated. With few exceptions, police have little training in dealing with any offender. Particularly among the black and the poor and within the inner city, the policeman is regarded as a punitive authority to be defeated. It will take considerable effort and time to change the image of the police in these areas, an image that is only too often reinforced by the police response to provocation with brutality. Thus, the policeman is considered an enemy, and shooting an enemy is a widely accepted practice. People feel free to decide who their enemy is, whether it is the Viet Cong or the police. They see no reason for a distinction and, consequently, the policemen are often the first victims of a civil war.

At the present time we do not deal with the issues that lead to crime. Often poor substitutes are used in the hope of ameliorating the situation. For example, there is a relationship between crime and cultural and economic deprivation; money alone, however, will not change the crime rate. Money will not change the concepts of the poor about their own status and role in society. Providing education will not help much, either, because our educational approaches are often inadequate, particularly in dealing with the underprivileged.

Education can and should play a major part in shaping our future society. Yet, at the present time, the influence of the school on the next generation is deplorably low. Conflict begins in grade school, becomes more intense in high school, and leads to the dissatisfaction of college students. Instead of providing the highest ideals for the elite of our youth, institutions of higher education are inviting rebellion because they are not democratic and because the curricula do not meet their students' needs. They need a fundamental revision.

Such a change in the structure and function of the university will have a considerable influence on high schools. It is on the high school level that the deficiencies in our educational system are most obvious. Under the pressure of deciding who has the right to go to college and who has not, the present pernicious method of grading cannot be eliminated. Yet if the purpose of going to college were merely to acquire more knowledge, one would not need any grades. Only those students who really want to learn would go to college—and they would go without the fear of failure that is systematically fostered in most universities.

LABOR–MANAGEMENT CONFLICTS

The conflict between labor and management constitutes another major source of friction, and, at present, there is little hope for any immediate solution.

Gradually, labor has gained power while management has lost it, but the fight between the two groups seems to be as permanent as the fight between two brothers. Few, indeed, think that the struggle will ever stop, despite the terrific price that labor and management pay for their "rights." Society sanctions the continued struggle by accepting the principle of bargaining, which means that both sides try to get as much as possible and to give as little as possible.

A case study sums up current industrial relations perfectly. The union studied the financial situation of the company and found that it could afford an increase of 7 percent in wages. The union knew it, and the company knew it. But in order to get 7 percent, the union felt that it had to demand 10 percent, and the company, in order to "give" 7 percent, offered 5 percent. If the union were to ask for 7 percent at the outset of negotiations, it would never get 7 percent; if the company offered 7 percent, it would end up paying more.

There is little indication that this process of outsmarting each other is recognized for its social significance. Both parties in the dirty game are obstructing progress and eventual social harmony. But let us go a little deeper into the subject to face the paranoic assumption that management has only one purpose: to control and defeat labor. (This does not mean that this assumption is not sometimes valid.)

Baritz gives a thorough account of the attitudes of labor and management.[1] What is so terrifying is the fact that he gives an exhaustive report of all the effective methods developed over the last 20 years to promote peace and understanding and then denounces them as schemes to enslave labor. We may guess from the many quotations he furnishes that he expresses widely accepted opinions, but if we believe him and those from whom he quotes, there is no chance of ever bringing peace and harmony into industry. Baritz therefore reinforces the widespread opinion that man is incapable of living in peace with his fellows.

The need for industrial peace is more than an economic necessity. Work is one of the fundamental tasks everyone has to fulfill. Work means making a useful contribution to society. It is more than a duty; it is part of man's function in life—and a very important one. If everyone would get enough money to satisfy all his needs, including luxuries, many probably would stop working—but for how long? At Alcatraz the most effective form of "punishment" was exclusion from work.

Working means more than making a living, and there is no need to be at war with one's boss or one's employees. Exploita-

---

1. Loren Baritz, *The Servants of Power* (Middletown, Conn.: Wesleyan University Press, 1960).

tion of one side by the other need not exist. In fact, working is too important an aspect of life to be controlled by people who exploit each other.

The conflicts at work are of the same nature as all the other conflicts of our time. They are based on competition, struggle for power, for increasing one's rights, and for disregarding the rights of others.

Since the end of World War II, great progress has been made because the traditional autocratic demand has proved to be sufficient to get results. Managers often overlooked the human element: they knew what to do with machines, but not with men. A great variety of psychological and social techniques were discovered to promote harmony and avoid conflicts. The most important discoveries are in the field of group dynamics. Frank discussions between all segments of industry —not merely between foremen and workers—can improve relationships and solve the problems that managers, foremen, and workers have. Role-playing effectively reveals underlying conflicts and grievances and helps to resolve them. Participation in decision-making creates mutual understanding and willingness to cooperate.

Many companies have found ways to achieve these results. Among the systematic procedures developed is the Motivation Hygiene Theory of Herzberg[2] and his many associates, which attempts to take into account the basic needs of man. It seems that a man's productive activity—his success and failure in his work—profoundly affects his moral state. Myers, an associate of Herzberg, raises the question: "What motivates employees to work effectively?" And he answers:

> A challenging job which allows feeling of achievement, responsibility, growth, advancement, enjoyment of work itself, and earned recognition.

2. Frederick Herzberg, *The Motivation to Work* (New York: Wiley & Sons, 1959).

What dissatisfies workers? Mostly factors which are peripheral to the job, work rules, lighting, coffee breaks, titles, seniority rights, wages, fringe benefits, and the like.

When do workers become dissatisfied? When opportunities for meaningful achievement are eliminated and they become sensitized to their environment and begin to find faults.[3]

According to Baritz, all efforts to create labor-peace are opposed by many labor spokesmen and sympathizers. One labor spokesman called the system of participation vicious; others, "at best paternalistic and at worst, despotic." Although the system of participation actually "converted radical workers into sound management-oriented employees," labor's conviction that democratic methods are bound to fail in industry is matched by an equally strong doubt on the part of management. In fact, the labor struggle is nòt only between labor and management—the class struggle that Marx envisioned—but also between worker and union, between worker and foreman, and between manager and manager.

The best scheme will not work as long as mutual distrust continues. Profit-sharing paid off in some instances; in others it did not, because the workers did not trust their employers to declare their profit honestly. Here we have the same situation: where there is fight and antagonism, nobody benefits. Only in a democratic transaction based on mutual respect can any one of the many conflicts in our society be resolved.

THE PROBLEM OF ECONOMICS

Our society is besieged by economic problems. No nation is free of them; no individual can ignore them. The fear of starvation and of deprivation and economic setbacks and their consequences is shared by all, without regard to their wealth.

---

3. M. Scott Myers, "Who Are Your Motivated Workers?" *Harvard Business Review*, Vol. 42, 1964.

Why have we failed to solve our economic problems—or at least to approach them with some well-defined program?

As in all other aspects where we struggle to find answers, we neglect the *human* element in economics. We are not even aware to what extent the human factor *affects* economics, the stock market, monetary upheavals, progress, or recession.

Fear and insecurity, success or failure, anticipation—all clearly have a strong effect on economic developments. Yet different theories contradict each other, and there is little understanding of the psychological dynamics that lead various economists to develop their own theories.

Many schemes have been offered for the solution of economic problems. Everyone sticks to his own ideas and does not want to attribute controlling influence to any other scheme.

We are in no position today to foresee what kind of economic system will ultimately come to best serve the needs of society and all of its members. No one knows whether the system will be a free or a controlled economy; it may well be a mixed economy, combining some elements of planning with some of free enterprise. A person's wealth may become as insignificant as his race, religion, or political persuasion. When individual qualities or achievements no longer determine superior status, we may find that we are able to accumulate wealth without receiving more benefit than those who collect stamps or antiques receive. Only in such a situation will we be ready to find a solution to our economic problems, which presently can cause unlimited hardships.

POLITICAL DEMOCRACY

Political democracy by itself does not insure the achievement of true equality. Despite the provisions of the Constitution, minority groups, women, and youth are still deprived of equal political rights.

The political conventions of both parties are typical examples of our brand of democracy. The right of every delegate to stop the procedures is hailed as a wonderful example of democracy. But when the chips are down and the decisions have to be made, the individual delegate, the little fellow, has very little to say. The "bosses" decide the issues among themselves.

This parody of democracy is, unfortunately, not limited to the political arena; it can be witnessed wherever powerful groups control institutions. Our institutionalism in its pernicious consequences has been particularly evident in organizations of every kind. In national organizations, in the field of social sciences, or in education, certain dominant groups often maintain a monopoly that is almost impossible to break. And all this control is exercised with an unbelievable capacity to maintain the *appearance* of democratic procedures. Railroading and extremely skillful manipulations by apparently scrupulous observation of the rules of order permit dominant groups to exert their control.

We all are aware of the accepted procedures that make our present "democracy" more objectionable than any ouright autocratic display of power. Autocracy, at least, is generally without hypocrisy. The pretense that inevitably results when democratic principles are proclaimed but not applied has brought the whole democratic way of life into disrepute. We have to become much clearer in our understanding and application of what democracy means before we will be able, through our own enthusiasm and conviction, to help others recognize the undeniable benefits of a democratic society.

We may have to revise our thinking about majority rule. The reliance on the majority, on *numbers*, precludes the ability to judge issues by their logical, moral, or intellectual value. If the majority *imposes* its will on the minority, the minority will only grudgingly accept the decision and fight it. Thus, we never reach agreement, only a shift of power.

As the principle of equal opportunity is a poor substitute

for real equality, so rule by majority is imposition. We take the majority principle for granted because we know of no better way of reconciling contrasting opinions and interests, but the reason for this deficiency is our lack of democratic leadership. Wherever such leadership exists, it makes its influence felt in the ability to negotiate and to clarify until a *common ground for action* is reached. We are accustomed to call that leadership quality "diplomacy," not without some contempt, because it has in the past been used mostly in dealing with power and power groups in a rather devious mode of operation. Skillful leadership does use diplomacy, but not in the traditional sense. Skillful leadership is the leadership a teacher needs to guide a discussion by her students, that parents need to win the support of their children, that the arbitrator needs to solve labor problems, and that the government agent needs to overcome racial antagonism.

Kurt Lewin demonstrated the importance of democratic leadership, which alone can produce. constructive group activities. This kind of leadership means more than conducting or leading a discussion. The democratic leader must be able to reconcile opposing interests and points of view, to bring about the consensus without which the democratic process cannot operate. The most urgent task in this moment of our history is to train competent leaders who do not impose their ideas on the group but help their followers to develop ideas and means of reaching agreement.

All parents and teachers need training in leadership if they want to regain their influence on children and youth. Such leadership is particularly needed if we will try—and we must—to encourage healthy encounters in our communities between the hostile and mutually antagonistic groups that threaten the peace of our whole country. Without leadership such meetings could not take place, and if they did, they would lead to more arguments and increased hostility. The collision course in which we find ourselves cannot be stopped without such leadership, particularly in moments of crisis and clash. The availability of such leaders in every community is a prerequisite for ending hostility and preventing reoccurence.

We need leaders of and for the young, leaders who are able to stimulate the development of concepts, attitudes, and particularly values. Only through group discussion can values be changed successfully, for the group is a value-forming agent. A trained teacher, who can use the group effectively, can change the moral values of her students.

The search for better values and meaning is probably felt everywhere, mostly among the youth, but also by adults. All need group participation for the establishment and maintenance of new values. An agent for such changes is religion. It concerns itself with fundamental values in living.

CHAPTER 13 · **The Function of Religion**

Man cannot stand alone. He can function and feel secure in his own strength only *within his group*. Society is the medium that he requires for living. Only if he is fully integrated into society can his needs be met. Close social integration requires emotional stimulation and emotional responses.

The emotional stimulation that evokes the best in each person is often called "spiritual." This term has been used to connote not only the divine but also the higher intellectual and moral motivations of which a human being is capable. Throughout man's history the most potent instrument for the satisfaction of his spiritual needs has been religion. In religious experience man has sought and found strong feelings of cohesion and belonging. Through religion man has been lifted above the tribulations of daily existence and been given a focus for the greater perspective of life. Thus religion has served the needs of the individual throughout the ages.

But religion has a function for society as well. Since its earliest organization society has sought to cultivate in its members attitudes that comply with its necessities. Every group has its own self-established conventions and standards. Accepting social regulations is mandatory for social living. In most societies religious prescriptions have affected the thought and action of all members. Religious rituals have evoked their emotions and integrated them into one group.

Today, when civilization tends to automatize its members, pitching man against man in endless competition, religion becomes of particular importance. But organized religion often fails to provide the intellectual content, the rituals, and the spiritual symbols that can serve the specific needs of democracy, with its egalitarian tendencies. Yet the fact that society's rebels, fighting against the Western establishment, are often eagerly exploring Eastern religions in search of a feeling of communality and joy seems to demonstrate a continuing need for a new religious experience.

Discussions of religion usually center on contemporary religions. Most definitions of religion reflect merely the view of particular creeds—in the Western world usually Christianity. Consequently, such definitions fail to take into account the broader aspects of the religious experience. Because religion has changed its meaning and content with each different culture, historical perspective can perhaps help us to recognize religion's essential function.

In primitive society religion was mystic. Since primitive society was strongly collective, primitive religion was predominantly collectivistic. The individual was closely integrated into his group. Primitive religion originated in clan or tribal consciousness. It had no place for an individual deity, since the individual was not conceived as such, but rather as a part of the group. When tribal collectivism began to break up and the individual emerged as an isolated particle in the heterogeneous social structure of civilization, individual deities likewise emerged. In contrast to the mysticism of the primitives, religion became deistic. It became a highly individualized experience.[4]

Primitive religion was concerned with natural forces; so were the religions in the early period of civilization. Then the emphasis shifted to social problems. With Greek culture, and especially the spread of the Orphic Mysteries, religion came to revolve around concepts of sin and of individual atone-

---

4. This description of the development of religion follows basically accepted evolutionary theories, particularly those proposed by Alfred Bartholet, *Kultur und Religion* (Göttingen, 1924).

ment. The concept of individual communion with the deity gained ascendancy, particularly as a result of dwindling state power in the late Hellenistic period. Individual deities behaved much as individuals did in society. To reach an all-inclusive social authority, society moved toward unified autocracy; so did its gods. One god won over his rivals in much the same fashion as did the strongest ruler in the formation of empires. Monotheism, created by Jews, with its emphasis on social order and justice, became the prevalent religious concept in the era of contested rule by power. Then came the trend toward democracy, away from the futile struggle for power and superiority. The Greek Stoics, under the influence of early Buddhism, formulated the idea of fundamental human equality; they were the first in the Western culture to develop a religion that we may term "modern." It deprived Zeus of his "divine" nature and identified him with the universal and imminent "reason" or logos. The pantheistic religion of the Stoics had no place for divinities and the supernatural.

Buddhism likewise discarded the metaphysics of Brahmanism and was "atheistic" in its original form. The "regression" of Buddhism from a simple formula for living to supernatural concepts characterized religion at the end of the ancient culture. A similar development can be observed in Christianity. The early Christians believed in and practiced human equality. The Savior was a man, a teacher, a human being. (It is interesting to note that Buddha, too, was considered by his later disciples to be a son of God.) The early democratic religious concepts corresponded with the trend that saw the beginning of a democratic social organization, but this trend ended with the collapse of the Roman Empire. Society regressed to an authoritarian, feudal political organization; Augustinian orthodoxy replaced the egalitarian spirit of the Christian faith. The term "rationalism" first appeared within the religious sphere during the Renaissance, together with the rediscovery of historical democratic concepts. Renaissance humanists were inspired by a revulsion for the medieval reliance on authority and the subordination of reason to it; they tried to vindicate the autonomy of reason over the authority of books and institutions. Reason was considered to possess in itself the capacity for all truths, including the religious and moral. The dogma of original sin, or corruption of reason through the fall of man, was rejected.

As modern society began to reject autocratic rule in favor of a relationship of equals, the reign of God as a symbol of supreme power protecting the right of earthly rulers to maintain their superiority over others was also challenged. Man, realizing his own value and dignity, deposed not only kings, emperors, and tyrants but also the divine aristocracy. Millions lost their belief in a personal god. Thus once again revolt against the supernatural coincided with the tendency toward democracy.

As the influence of organized religion diminished, many found themselves lost, without guidance and direction. Others turned for stimulation and direction to group movements. Nationalism and political and ideological movements of various kinds replaced religion by offering stimulations for devotion, cooperation, and integration. But these movements fail because they are essentially divisive. No ideology has so far provided an all-inclusive philosophy for daily life in our culture.

A RELIGION FOR DEMOCRACY

Democracy traditionally questions the existence of the supernatural, but this does not mean that democracy abhors religion. The "spiritual needs" of mankind do not require the existence of supernatural powers. Men still demand an orientation that, on the one hand, can lift individuals out of their daily isolation and perpetuate the higher values in their lives and, on the other, can provide society with a channel for communicating its concepts and perspectives, its morals and values. Each cultural period in the past has found its appropriate religion; it is safe to assume that the cultural epoch of democracy will also find its religious expression. To be sure, this new and universal religion does not yet exist, and no one can say what it will be like. But certain aspects of the democratic religion are already becoming clear.

The new religion will be humanistic. It will be concerned with man and not with god. The concept of a personal god, of a power outside our natural existence, of supernatural forces, does not fit our way of life; nor does it suit individuals who are aware of their independence and self-determination, of the strength and force within themselves.

Its truth will be empirical. This truth will be of a fundamentally different nature from that that previous generations and cultures visualized. There will be no dogmatic assertion of "absolute truth," no scientific attempts to "discover" truth. We can find only approximations of truth; relativity will replace absolutes.

The prescriptions of the new religion will serve new morals. As new moral values emerge in the democratic evolution, many hallowed concepts will crumble. The change in our standards of behavior will be reflected in our structure of moral values. Personal ambition, righteousness, a strong sense of duty, conformity, perfectionism, and similar qualities that are stimulated and esteemed in our society are no longer sufficient to motivate free men to do their best; these values often become the source of failure and deficiency. It is no longer sufficient to be good and successful. Fulfillment of one's own life, living in peace and harmony with one's fellow man—and with oneself—may require considerable modification of established codes. Instead of ambition, we may need enthusiasm; instead of righteousness, friendliness and understanding; instead of a sense of obligation, a sense of belonging, empathy, and participation. Mere conformity will not stimulate improvement; courage to be imperfect will prove healthier and more beneficial than perfectionism.

The new religion will provide new symbols. Perhaps the greatest deficiency of modern humanism is that it has failed to provide effective and generally accepted symbols. Symbols are signposts that evoke specific personal attitudes. They are shortcuts in persuasion and motivation. They arouse almost automatic responses from those who accept them. Symbols do not require explanations because they are understood. They are necessary for group cohesion and group movement. Any new religion will need symbols because without them it cannot be a social force.

We can only speculate on what kind of symbols will emerge. But we can be fairly certain that the basic symbol of orthodox religions—the concept of sin—will be absent. Sin is the embodiment of all that is evil, all that should be avoided. But the concept of sin requires an authority to declare what sin is. Sin is an atavism in a democratic social organization. People act badly not because of their sinful makeup but because they are misguided. They are not "bad" but discouraged. Whoever is wrong or "bad" needs help, understanding, and treatment, not condemnation or punishment. Punishment has lost its effectiveness as a corrective procedure in a democratic era, where no one, not even a child, can be *forced* to behave properly.

Fear of punishment was an integral part of orthodox religion. The threat of punishment on this earth and in the hereafter was designed to create fear as a deterrent to transgression. But today fear has become the greatest obstacle to fulfillment and function, to self-respect and self-realization. In contrast, courage is one of the requirements for freedom. Modern man needs courage to face uncertainties since certainty is assured only in an autocracy. Modern man needs courage because he recognizes his own spontaneity and creativeness—and it requires courage to be spontaneous. Only a courageous person who knows his strength and has faith in himself can have faith in others; only such a person can accept the give and take of social living. A new religion, whatever other symbols it needs, will need a symbol that evokes courage, belief in one's own strength and ability.

The new religion will provide a new ritual. The new religious ritual will consist of mutual help. The spiritual and moral support we all need in the discouraging tribulations of our daily lives can only come from a group in which we are truly one another's brothers. We need each other's help in our efforts to be as good as we want to be, to be as effective as we can. We need each other to remind us of our ideals and to give us persistence in pursuing them. We need each other to stimulate our devotion to the common good, to stir up our willingness to feel with each other, to live with each other, to belong to each other in a long-delayed fulfillment of humanity's most cherished and ancient dream: the brotherhood of man.